**FOR MY DAD, WHO STARTED PATIENTLY ANSWERING
MY SCIENCE QUESTIONS AS SOON AS I COULD TALK –
AND HASN'T STOPPED SINCE – T.W**

FOR BRIG – J.D

First published 2020 by Walker Books Ltd
87 Vauxhall Walk, London SE11 5HJ

2 4 6 8 10 9 7 5 3 1

This book has been typeset in Sabon, Intro Black and Amasis

Printed and bound in UK

British Library Cataloguing in Publication Data: a catalogue record
for this book is available from the British Library

ISBN 978-1-4063-8825-1

www.walker.co.uk

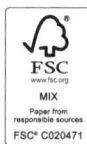

WALKER
BOOKS

FSC
www.fsc.org
MIX
Paper from
responsible sources
FSC® C020471

GET AHEAD IN...

CHEMISTRY

GET AHEAD IN....

CHEMISTRY

from the
PERIODIC TABLE
to the
APOCALYPSE

ILLUSTRATED BY
TOM WHIPPLE JAMES DAVIES

CONTENTS

INTRODUCTION

Do I really need another Chemistry textbook?

You don't. The one you have is fine.
I'm sure it covers everything you
need for your exams. And yet...

And yet what?

Well, I'm sure it tells you, say, in the
Acids and Alkalis chapter, that:

Acids are characterised by the concentration of H+ ions.

Alkalis are characterised by OH- ions.

Acids and bases react to form salts and water.

That's all correct, and all stuff you need to know.

Great, so I'll just reread it.

You could, of course. But let's be honest – it's hard.

Chemistry is a wonderful subject. It's about how the building blocks of the planet around us come together to make the wondrous complexity of everything we see. It is vital to understanding the world.

It is also, just sometimes, very difficult.

And this book isn't?

I hope not. For instance, that stuff about $H+$ ions? It's the reason why a Danish scientist was able to save two Nobel medals – and why Cleopatra was able to host the world's most expensive dinner party.

I think the science is easier to remember, once you've heard the amazing stories behind it.

What about $OH-$ ions? Can you glam them up, too?

Well ... if you're a Roman general, you can use $OH-$ ions to blind your enemies?

Is this really useful to know?

Yes! Because the mechanisms involved might just explain a bit of the Chemistry you need to know for your exams.

So this book is useful because it includes stories about lavish dinner parties and sadistic generals?

Yes!

Um, not just that. There are also lusty turkeys, fart-filled balloons ... and the possibility that chemists could trigger an alien invasion, and the destruction of all life on Earth.

Where are you going with this?

The point is, this book is not meant to be a replacement for a revision guide. It's meant to be an assistant to one.

It tells you how we got to where we are, and why – and hopefully, along the way, will help you to remember the most important details.

Details like?

Well, Avogadro's constant is technically $6.02214086 \times 10^{23}$ mol^{-1}

It's also the reason why scientists have made the smoothest object in the world: a shiny black sphere.

And it's *so* smooth that, if it were a planet the size of Earth, the distance between the deepest ocean and tallest mountain would be 5 metres.

Will there still be equations, as well as weirdly mesmeric spheres?

Not many. Certainly, not as many as you'll find in your textbook.

Each chapter is tied, though, to a key topic for learning Chemistry. By the end, you will have covered the whole syllabus – building on and deepening the knowledge you already have.

Great! So I can forget the equations.

No, definitely not. Textbooks – and teachers! – are very useful. They have a lot of information that they need to pass on.

Sometimes, in doing so, it isn't always possible to share the stories of the people behind that information: the women and men who saw further, thought deeper, worked harder or (to give another example) used Chemistry to destroy a nearby village.

That's where this book comes in.

So, onto Chapter One – which means it's time for aliens…

CHAPTER 1

THE PERIODIC TABLE

INTRODUCTION
THE PERIODIC TABLE

IN THIS CHAPTER YOU WILL LEARN ABOUT:

- Atoms, what they are made of and how they are different from each other
- Elements, which are substances made from one type of atom
- The Periodic Table, which orders the elements
- The families of elements, which behave in similar ways
- Compounds, which are atoms that are chemically joined together

BEFORE YOU READ THIS CHAPTER:

What is stuff? What is in the wood of a door that you knock on, or the bone of the knuckles that rap against it? What is it that makes water watery, or oranges orange?

What are the bricks from which the universe is constructed?

The world around us is not, it turns out, made from one kind of brick.

The building blocks that make up the glass of a skyscraper's windows are not the same as those in the steel struts that hold it in place.

And the blocks in a Lego brick are not the same as those in a real brick.

Instead, just like in Lego, there are lots of different bricks in our world, each used to make the different intricate structures we call "matter" – everything from the black carbon in your pencil to the unstable uranium in an atomic bomb.

In this chapter, we will look at how these bricks, known as atoms, relate to each other. This is the longest chapter, and also the one you may find the hardest – but it is important because it sets up everything that is to come.

It is about the elements: what makes one different from another, what makes groups of them similar and how finding the hidden order, which links them all together, led to the birth of modern Chemistry.

At the end of the book, there's a detailed Periodic Table you can refer back to – as well as information on the different "groups".

THE PERIODIC TABLE

Douglas Vakoch is the human in charge of making contact with aliens.

It's not an easy job. To communicate with another civilization, you have to have a shared language; you have to have knowledge in common. But these are aliens.

Vakoch, head of the organization Messaging Extraterrestrial Intelligence, thinks he knows what our shared language is. When he finally receives the confirmation he can go ahead and transmit, he will beam a powerful radio signal that he has already prepared out towards our cosmic neighbours.

That message, sent in 1s and 0s, is intended to be unmistakable to anyone who understands science. Starting with hydrogen, ending with oganesson, it is an encoding of the **elements** (the building blocks of the world around us), in order.

It is something called the **Periodic Table.**

Why that particular message? There are very few common reference points we would have with aliens, but the elements are one.

DOUGLAS VAKOCH

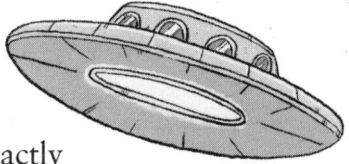

Iron on Alpha Centauri is the same as iron in Droitwich. Hydrogen on Planet X does exactly the same things that hydrogen does on Planet Earth.

Showing we understand these elements, and how they are organized in the universe, will – in his view! – be our way of announcing our entry into the cosmic community.

It tells other civilizations we are clever, sophisticated and ready to chat.

So, why hasn't he sent it already?

It is not because any scientist seriously doubts that an advanced alien civilization would know about the elements. It is because there is something of a debate (to put it mildly) about whether it is still sensible to let aliens know we're here.

Martin Dominik, an astronomer from St Andrew's University, points out that it may not be a good idea to tell super intelligent aliens where we are.

"Some say this is the greatest thing we should do," writes Dominik. "Some think we should be very quiet, and this should be the last thing we should do … and it might indeed be the last thing we *will* do."

How so?

"Maybe," he says, "they will come and eat us."

ORIGIN STORIES

All great scientific discoveries need their own legend.

With Newton's discovery of gravity, the story is that his inspiration arrived in the form of a falling apple. With Archimedes' discovery of displacement, it's that the solution came to him in the bath – prompting him to leap out and run down the street yelling "Eureka!"

The discovery of the Periodic Table is important enough that it has two legends.

According to one account, it came about because Dmitri Mendeleev, a nineteenth-century Russian, made a special set of cards.

Mendeleev, a professor working to improve Russia's chemical industry, had become obsessed with how to put the **elements** in the correct logical order.

When he went on long train journeys, he brought along a pack of 63 cards containing all the known elements, from hydrogen to bismuth. Then he would try to arrange them correctly – whatever that might mean! – in a game of "chemical solitaire".

Eventually, on a visit where he was meant to be inspecting a cheese factory (a task he was clearly less interested in than playing cards), the solitaire produced the order of the elements.

According to another account, it was not the cards that gave him the answer, but his subconscious.

After years of obsessing, he fell asleep one day and, "In a dream I saw a table where all the elements fell into place as required. Awakening, I immediately wrote it down on a piece of paper."

Whether one, or both, stories are really true is less important than what it is they tell us.

The first tells us that this table is a logical ordering: that the disordered elements prior to it were a problem to be solved.

The second tells us that its discovery is just that: a discovery, not an invention.

Chemists argue that the Periodic Table contains a fundamental truth of nature ... as eternally true as that 100 is 10 squared.

That is why they think, if you went into a Chemistry lesson on an alien planet, the elements would have different names – but they would still be there, lined up in the same groups, in the same way, on the same faded diagram on the wall.

The Periodic Table is not just "a" way of organizing Chemistry. It is "the" way of organising Chemistry.

To understand why, you need to first understand the things it contains: elements.

But to understand *elements*, you need to first understand the things they contain: *atoms*.

PERIODIC TABLE OF ELEMENTS

GROUPS

Atomic number → (2) **H** Helium

Element symbol
Element name

1	2		3	4	5	6	7	0
1 **H** Hydrogen								2 **He** Helium
3 **Li** Lithium	4 **Be** Beryllium		5 **B** Boron	6 **C** Carbon	7 **N** Nitrogen	8 **O** Oxygen	9 **F** Fluorine	10 **Ne** Neon
11 **Na** Sodium	12 **Mg** Magnesium		13 **Al** Aluminium	14 **Si** Silicon	15 **P** Phosphorus	16 **S** Sulphur	17 **Cl** Chlorine	18 **Ar** Argon

1	2	3	4	5	6	7	8	9	10	11	12	3	4	5	6	7	0
19 **K** Potassium	20 **Ca** Calcium	21 **Sc** Scandium	22 **Ti** Titanium	23 **V** Vanadium	24 **Cr** Chromium	25 **Mn** Manganese	26 **Fe** Iron	27 **Co** Cobalt	28 **Ni** Nickel	29 **Cu** Copper	30 **Zn** Zinc	31 **Ga** Gallium	32 **Ge** Germanium	33 **As** Arsenic	34 **Se** Selenium	35 **Br** Bromine	36 **Kr** Krypton
37 **Rb** Rubidium	38 **Sr** Strontium	39 **Y** Yttrium	40 **Zr** Zirconium	41 **Nb** Niobium	42 **Mo** Molybdenum	43 **Tc** Technetium	44 **Ru** Ruthenium	45 **Rh** Rhodium	46 **Pd** Palladium	47 **Ag** Silver	48 **Cd** Cadmium	49 **In** Indium	50 **Sn** Tin	51 **Sb** Antimony	52 **Te** Tellurium	53 **I** Iodine	54 **Xe** Xenon
55 **Cs** Caesium	56 **Ba** Barium	57-71 **Lanthanides**	72 **Hf** Hafnium	73 **Ta** Tantalum	74 **W** Tungsten	75 **Re** Rhenium	76 **Os** Osmium	77 **Ir** Iridium	78 **Pt** Platinum	79 **Au** Gold	80 **Hg** Mercury	81 **Tl** Thallium	82 **Pb** Lead	83 **Bi** Bismuth	84 **Po** Polonium	85 **At** Astatine	86 **Rn** Radon
87 **Fr** Francium	88 **Ra** Radium	89-103 **Actinides**	104 **Rf** Rutherfordium	105 **Db** Dubnium	106 **Sg** Seaborgium	107 **Bh** Bohrium	108 **Hs** Hassium	109 **Mt** Meitnerium	110 **Ds** Darmstadtium	111 **Rg** Roentgenium	112 **Cn** Copernicium	113 **Nh** Nihonium	114 **Fl** Flerovium	115 **Mc** Moscovium	116 **Lv** Livermorium	117 **Ts** Tennessine	118 **Og** Oganesson

	3	4	5	6	7										
57 **La** Lanthanum	58 **Ce** Cerium	59 **Pr** Praseodymium	60 **Nd** Neodymium	61 **Pm** Promethium	62 **Sm** Samarium	63 **Eu** Europium	64 **Gd** Gadolinium	65 **Tb** Terbium	66 **Dy** Dysprosium	67 **Ho** Holmium	68 **Er** Erbium	69 **Tm** Thulium	70 **Yb** Ytterbium	71 **Lu** Lutetium
89 **Ac** Actinium	90 **Th** Thorium	91 **Pa** Protactinium	92 **U** Uranium	93 **Np** Neptunium	94 **Pu** Plutonium	95 **Am** Americium	96 **Cm** Curium	97 **Bk** Berkelium	98 **Cf** Californium	99 **Es** Einsteinium	100 **Fm** Fermium	101 **Md** Mendelevium	102 **No** Nobelium	103 **Lr** Lawrencium

THE ATOM, AND WHY THE PERIODIC TABLE WORKS

When Mendeleev was creating the Periodic Table, chemists did not have the skills to explain why it worked: they just knew that it did.

The deeper truth it exposed was, ultimately, the very nature of matter itself.

At the time, scientists thought that the smallest thing you could have was the atom – a minute "particle", a chemical speck of dust that defined a substance.

Then, for each element they found, there was a different, indivisible, atom.

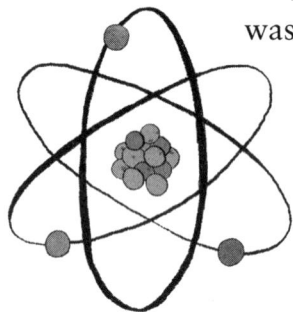

An atom, we now know, is not the smallest thing after all. It is made of three smaller things, known as **protons, neutrons** and **electrons**.

More than that, these same particles appear in all elements,[*1] they just appear in different quantities. (That's not the whole story – see p. 232 for more details, and watch out for the other numbered footnotes.)

An atom of carbon, which is the black stuff in your pencil, is not so different from an atom of oxygen, which is the gassy stuff you breathe.

Carbon has six of each of the protons, neutrons and electrons; oxygen has eight of each.

For the purpose of simplicity,[*2] we like to think of an atom as a central clump, called a nucleus, containing neutrons and positively-charged protons – both of which weigh about the same.

Around this orbit negatively-charged electrons, which weigh almost nothing.

There are as many electrons as protons, so their charges cancel each other out ... and the atom itself is neither positively charged, nor negatively charged.

In this miniature Solar System, the electrons have orbits – just like planets. In Chemistry, we call each "orbit" a "shell".

But the shells get full quickly. For example: there isn't room for Earth and Mars to circle the Sun at the same distance; the same rule applies to electrons.

Just two electrons can fit in the first shell.

If an atom has any more electrons, it has to fill up the second one – which is farther away, and can have eight.

The next shell also accepts up to eight electrons.[*3]

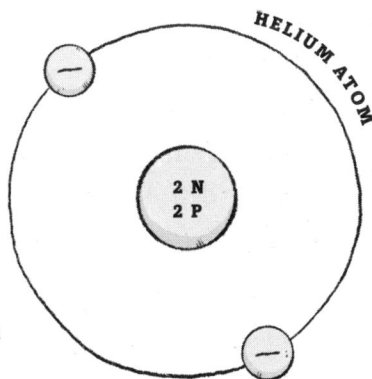

HELIUM ATOM

2 N
2 P

KEY:
N = Neutron
P = Proton
⊝ = Electron

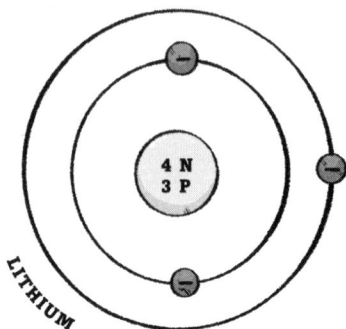
LITHIUM

This means that lithium, with three electrons, has its first shell full and one electron in the second.

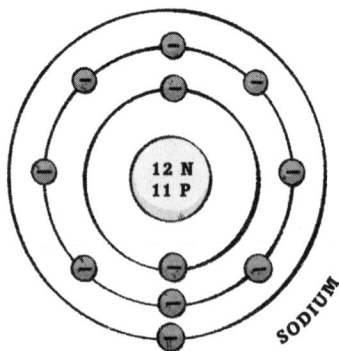
SODIUM

Meanwhile sodium, which has eleven electrons, has its first two shells full, then one electron in its third.

ELEMENTS

An element is a substance made up from one single type of atom – not that Mendeleev, at the time, really understood what an atom was.

And the elements are to Chemistry what species are to Biology.

Biologists group species into families: so, for instance, a tiger, lion and cheetah are put together with other felines, such as your fat and rather less ferocious tabby cat. And a shark and a goldfish are put together with other things that have fins and gills, known as "fish".

In the same way, Chemistry likes to organize its elements. The question for Mendeleev was: how?

For centuries before Mendeleev, people had been discovering and trying to make sense of the elements.

The first elements to be found in their pure form were the metals: gold, silver, copper, lead. All became crucial to the economies of the ancients. One, iron, was so important that it defined a new era: the Iron Age.

By the early nineteenth century, far more exotic elements were being added to this list. In a race between the laboratories of the world, chemists competed to find new substances, and gain the honour of naming them.

Soon, there was a new element every year: vanadium, beryllium, tantalum, niobium.

But this was not Chemistry, it was stamp collecting. It was like discovering a tiger and not knowing it was very similar to a lion. And it was clear there was a pattern to be found.

The elements had different "**properties**", meaning that they looked different or behaved differently.

Some were metals, and they were shiny and conducted electricity.

Some were gases and never reacted – meaning that they never joined up with other atoms.

Some set on fire in contact with water, some didn't even tarnish.

In his dream, or maybe on his train journey, Mendeleev noticed a pattern.

If you ordered the elements from lightest to heaviest – and after every seven, went on to a new line (like a typewriter reaching the end of the paper!) – the columns seemed to share properties.

Sometimes, to make the elements line up correctly, Mendeleev left gaps for elements he believed had not yet been found – in a supreme act of confidence.

These were later filled by newly-discovered elements. And, to Mendeleev's original 63-element table, there have now been added more than 50 other elements.

Eventually he created a column "zero" to fit in the **noble gases** – a group of very unreactive gases – none of which had been discovered at the time.

These columns, or "groups" tell us important things.

Let's go back to the idea of "animal families"; for

biologists, there are the mammals, which give birth to live young [*4] and lactate. So too for chemists there are the **group 1** elements, which are soft, reactive and not very dense.

Biologists have the reptiles, which are cold-blooded and scaly. Chemists have the **group 0** elements, which are unreactive, gaseous and won't set on fire.

And so on!

CHEATING

Mendeleev's table didn't quite work perfectly. Sometimes, worryingly, he had to fiddle it a bit.

He swapped around iodine and tellurium, for instance, because, even though their weights implied otherwise, he wanted iodine in the same group as fluorine and chlorine. Iodine, fluorine and chlorine all behave in a similar way – with low melting and boiling points.

Although Mendeleev didn't know it at the time, there's an elegant reason for this – which speaks to an even deeper truth about the atom.

Because, really, the table should have been ordered by "**atomic number**" instead of **mass** – by the number of protons in an atom's nucleus.

But of course, Mendeleev had no idea then that atoms contained other particles.

MASS NUMBER

"Mass" is another word for "weight"* – and the mass of a hydrogen atom is $1.6737236 \times 10^{-24}$ g, while the mass of a carbon atom is $1.992646547 \times 10^{-23}$ g.

This is very small. Very small indeed.

If you write out the first number in full, it is 0.0000000000000000000000016737236 g.

And if you had a hydrogen atom for every person on the Earth, and you had a THOUSAND Earths, between them all you would still only have a thousandth of the mass of a dust particle.

These are not, it has to be said, the easiest numbers to work with. So chemists don't.

Instead, they use **mass number**: the number of neutrons and protons each atom has. Since the two particles weigh the same, and electrons basically weigh nothing, this more or less works.

* Or, technically (since that last sentence would make both your Chemistry and Physics teachers' heads explode), mass on the surface of the Earth is the same as weight. In space you can be weightless, but still have mass.

More importantly, it is also a lot easier. Under this system carbon is 12, hydrogen is 1, oxygen is 16 – and suddenly things are a lot simpler! [*5]

And this is what Mendeleev stumbled upon. Sodium and lithium, despite having different weights, behave in similar ways; so they do belong within the same "group" in the Periodic Table.

The reason why – a reason Mendeleev could not have known when he intuitively started a new line in his revolutionary table [*6] – is that they both have one electron in their outer shell.

Elements in **group 2** have *two* in their outer shell, **group 3** have *three* – and so on.

It is these **outer-shell**, or "**valence**", electrons that determine a lot about how an element behaves. In particular, how reactive it is.

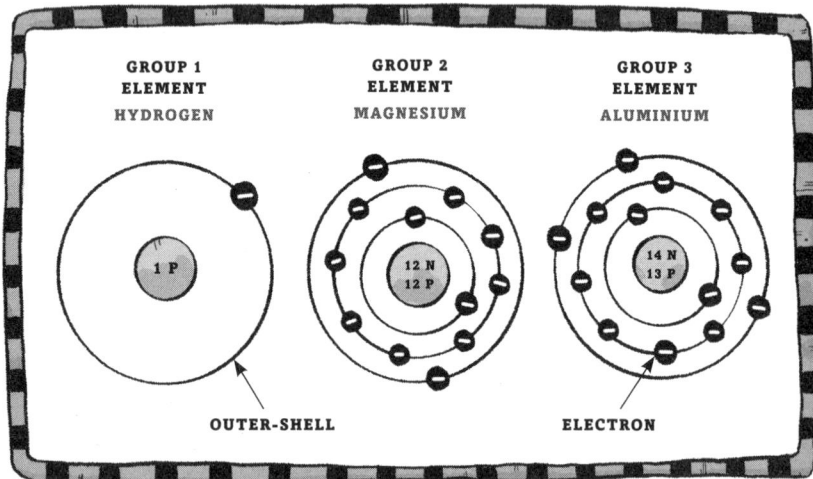

| GROUP 1 ELEMENT | GROUP 2 ELEMENT | GROUP 3 ELEMENT |
| HYDROGEN | MAGNESIUM | ALUMINIUM |

1 P

12 N 12 P

14 N 13 P

OUTER-SHELL

ELECTRON

PROPERTIES OF ELEMENTS

What are an element's **properties**? Really, that's another way of asking: what does it do that's interesting?

For instance, if you put a lump of potassium in water, it becomes very interesting indeed. It fizzes, burns lilac, and shoots off bits of itself.

And, once the show is over, the potassium atoms will have joined with some of the hydrogen and oxygen atoms in water to make potassium hydroxide.

But if you put a lump of iron in water, it's less interesting. It just goes rusty – very, very slowly.

And gradually, over time, the iron atoms join with oxygen ones to make iron oxide.

In both cases, one element is joining with another: which is to say, it is **"reacting"**.

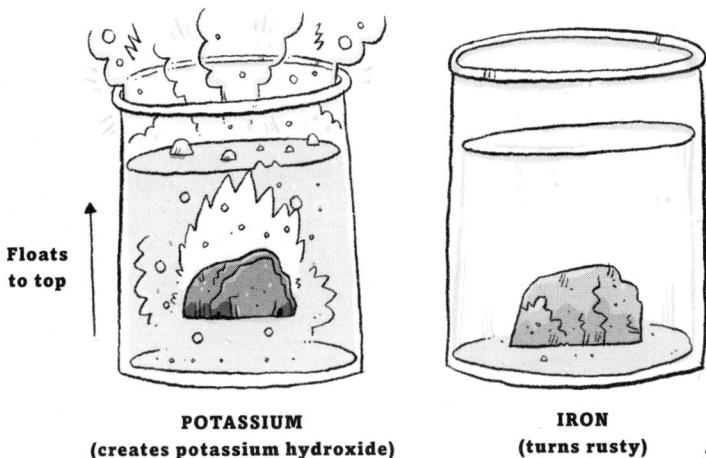

Floats to top

POTASSIUM
(creates potassium hydroxide)

IRON
(turns rusty)

31

Reactions are not the *only* interesting things that elements do.

For example, if you stick your fingers in a plug socket (don't do this) you will jiggle about, your hair will stand on end, and after a bit you'll probably die. And that's because copper, another element, is being interesting.

One of its properties is that it conducts electricity – in this case from power stations, through wires, and into you.

The third interesting thing which we're (um) interested in, is at what point an element boils or melts.

For instance, iron has been used throughout history to make swords – because it's generally found in a solid form. If it wasn't solid, you would have a pretty rubbish sword.

But if you heat iron up to temperatures just about achievable by humans, it will soften and melt. Otherwise, you wouldn't be able to make a sword out of it in the first place.

On some other planet, oxygen might make a really good sword (instead of a

really good gas to breathe, as it does on Earth). It's just that, to get oxygen cold enough that it turns solid, that planet would have to be 150 degrees Celsius colder than the South Pole in winter.

When elements change to liquids or gas is a very useful property to understand, if only because it prevents the embarrassing mistake of making swords out of thin air.

RAREST ELEMENTS

Some elements can be very hard to find. Take, for instance, promethium – element 61.

This element is named after Prometheus, a mythical Greek figure who was chained to the top of a mountain. Every night, an eagle tore out his liver. Every day, it regenerated: ready for the punishment to resume.

The name is appropriate. The reason there is estimated to be so little promethium – so little, in fact, that it has never been found in nature – is that it is very unstable. It is made when uranium, which is also unstable, decays. As soon as the promethium appears though, its atom wants to split apart into smaller ones – and does.

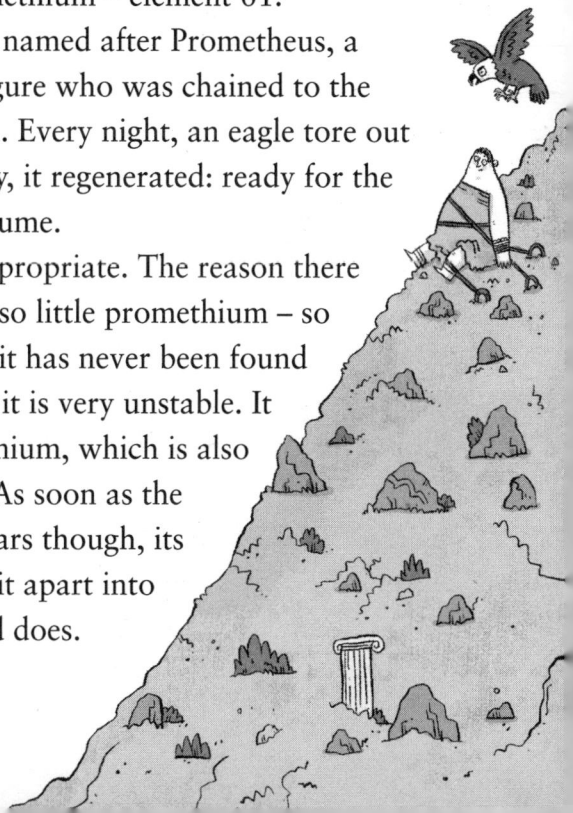

But at the same time, more promethium is manufactured in uranium as a replacement; just as with Prometheus's liver.

All of which means that, at any one point, the Earth contains about 500 g of this element ... or, roughly the weight of a liver.

COMPOUNDS

Most of the world is not just made of elements; it is made of elements joined together with other elements. From the H_2O of the water in the sea to the NaCl of the salt dissolved in it, our planet is composed of compounds.

There will be a lot more about compounds in the next chapter, but for now it is just worth realizing that the way that two elements join is determined by their Periodic Table group.

Oxygen, for instance, is **group 6**. That means it is two electrons short of a full shell of eight. And potassium is **group 1**: it has just one electron in its second shell.

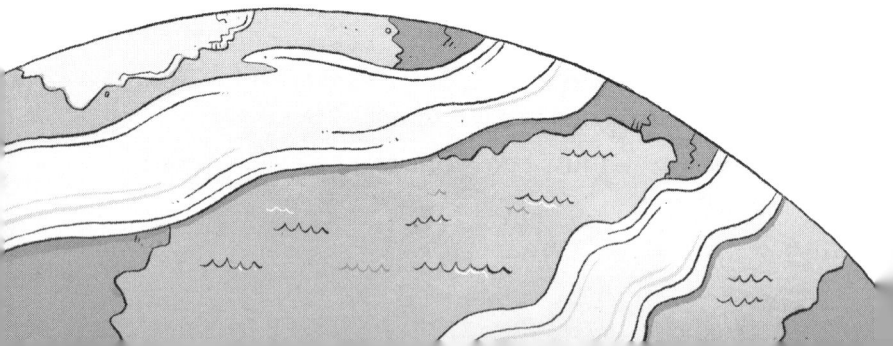

Put them together and they will unite to form a single compound composed of two potassium ions for every one oxygen – making potassium oxide.

Each oxygen atom has been loaned the spare electron from the two potassium atoms to complete its own shell.

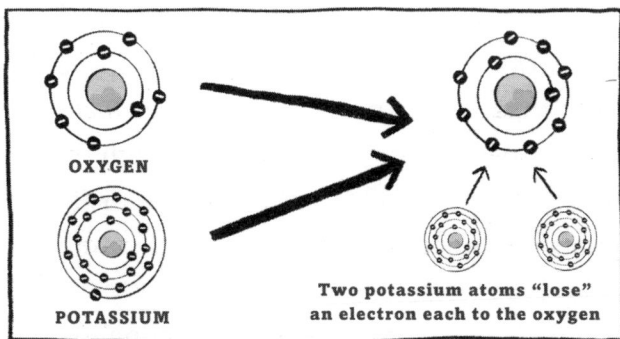

OXYGEN

POTASSIUM

Two potassium atoms "lose" an electron each to the oxygen

Why would the potassium atoms want to loan the spare electrons in their outer shell? Why are those electrons even "spare"? Why, in other words, do atoms prefer to have their shells full?

Why, for that matter, does the meaning of a "full" shell change – with two electrons in the first shell and eight in the next two?

Well, really, you need to stop thinking about atoms as miniature Solar Systems and (see page 230) start thinking of them as empty spaces filled with fuzzy wave functions in weird non-orbital shells.

Or you could just take your teacher's word for it.

ISOTOPES

In 1988, a representative of the Vatican took a knife and cut out a corner of one of the holiest objects in the Catholic Church: the Turin Shroud. Then he sent portions of it to three laboratories.

The Turin Shroud is, to believers, the image of Jesus. It is a simple piece of linen, made from plants (like any other piece of linen) – but it was the sheet used to wrap Jesus after his death. The ghostly face you can now see imprinted on it is, therefore, the face of the son of God himself.

But is it really over 2,000 years old? One way to find out is through historical records.

We know the shroud has been kept in Turin for 500 years. Before that, the earliest record is a sighting in Constantinople in 1204 – a Crusader knight claimed to have seen "the Shroud in which our Lord had been wrapped", while he was busy plundering a church.

But historical records aren't all that accurate. There is something more reliable, though, and that something is carbon – specifically, it is carbon isotopes.

An element is defined by the number of protons it has. The number of neutrons, though, can change.

Isotopes are atoms from the same element which have a different number of neutrons. So, for instance, the most common form of carbon has six protons and six neutrons. It is known as **carbon-12**, because its atomic mass is 12 (6 protons + 6 neutrons).

There are other forms of carbon, though. There is, for instance, carbon-13, with seven neutrons. There is also a rarer form called carbon-14, with 8.

All these carbons behave much like carbon. That means that they join with oxygen to make carbon dioxide, they get taken in by plants during photosynthesis, and they are then used by the plants to build up their stalks and leaves.

But don't be fooled: they are not the same.

Carbon-12 is the carbon you see everywhere. It is the carbon so reliable, so stable, that it makes up diamonds – and diamonds, as the James Bond film pointed out, are forever.

Not so carbon-14; it's flighty. Carbon-14 is made in the upper atmosphere, when a super-fast particle from the Sun collides with a nitrogen atom ... and it isn't built to last. Instead, it decays – releasing radiation then changing to a different element completely: nitrogen.

This process isn't fast. If, somehow, you had a pencil lead made out of carbon-14, it wouldn't suddenly disappear. It would take centuries, probably, before you noticed any change. But after a few tens of thousands of years, the graphite in your pencil would have completely changed into another element – nitrogen, as it happens.

And this is why carbon-14 is so useful. Because the same thing that happens in your pencil happens in plants. The tiny proportion of the carbon they take in, that was carbon-14, slowly disappears, while carbon-12 doesn't.

This means that you can measure the ratio of carbon-14 to carbon-12 in a sample of plant matter – such as a shroud – and work out how old it is. The less carbon-14 there is compared to carbon-12,

the longer it has been hanging around.

That is what each of those laboratories did, with their tiny corner of the shroud. They then sent the Vatican the results: it dated from the 1300s.

Not only could it not have been wrapped around the dead body of Jesus, it couldn't even have been the one seen in 1204.

All of which goes to show – don't trust a knight in search of booty.

MASS NUMBER (AGAIN!)

Atomic mass is a way of making things simpler. Instead of using really long and confusing numbers to give the weight of an atom of an element, it means you can use single whole numbers and compare them easily.

Well, why then is the atomic mass of carbon in the Periodic Table officially given as 12.0107?

The answer is isotopes. The Periodic Table gives the average mass, and most carbon in the world is carbon-12. But a small amount is carbon-13, and an even smaller amount is carbon-14.

Together, this means the average weight of all the atoms is a little more than 12.

WHAT IF YOU HAD A REAL PERIODIC TABLE?

The Periodic Table is a wonderful discovery. Wouldn't it be great if instead of merely being a poster on Chemistry classroom walls, it existed in reality?

Wouldn't it be a lovely gesture if, in honour of Mendeleev, someone built one out of the real substances – a jar of hydrogen, a glass of mercury, a chunk of iron, all in the correct places?

No actually, it wouldn't. It would destroy the world.

Only the first 92 elements exist in nature. The rest can only be made artificially, created in tiny quantities inside laboratories, generally by bashing particles together.

Even then, many only exist for a few seconds or less, before disappearing in a puff of energy. (Which sounds a lot less dramatic than it is.)

If you built a small Periodic Table out of the actual elements it represents, fashioning carbon, iron and the rest into bricks and putting them on the wall, you would have a beautiful creation.

But you wouldn't have much time to appreciate it, before the blast from the heavier elements created a mushroom cloud several kilometres in the air, spreading little bits of you throughout the stratosphere.

The good news is, before you got to the really dangerous elements that create nuclear explosions, you would have been killed by the ones that are merely highly toxic.

IN SHORT: It's all element-ary. (Which is to say, quite complex.)

WHAT YOU NEED TO KNOW

- Atoms are made of a nucleus of neutrons and positively-charged protons, orbited by negatively-charged electrons.
- An atom is the smallest unit of an element, and each element has a symbol – for instance zinc is Zn.
- Each element can have isotopes with different numbers of neutrons in their atoms. The element is defined by how many protons it has.
- An element's atomic number is its number of protons; its mass number is its number of protons and neutrons. So, the number of neutrons is the mass number minus the atomic number.
- A compound is chemically-bonded atoms of different elements.
- The Periodic Table is a way of ordering the elements in rows, from least number of protons to most.
- The group number, which is the column the element is in, relates to how many electrons are in its outermost shell. Elements in the same group have similar properties.
- In the Periodic Table, metals are on the left, non-metals on the right. Metals generally have a high melting point, non-metals generally don't.

Chemistry really can change the world. Discover how in TIME-TRAVELLING CHEMISTRY: there's a new instalment at t[h]e end of each chapter!

TIME-TRAVELLING CHEMISTRY

Time behaves differently during double Chemistry on a Friday afternoon. Each movement of the clock on the wall takes twice as long.

Your eye glances over the row of colourless chemicals in front of you. You like Chemistry: you're good at it. But you're also bored. Very, very, bored.

In front of you, Clare flicks a spitball at your ear.

You ignore her: she always flicks spitballs. Clare, who is annoyingly good at Chemistry, is also very annoying.

Then one bottle catches your eye. Between the ammonia and the hydrochloric acid there is one that you haven't seen before. It has no name. It just says, "DO NOT MIX WITH WATER".

You look to the front, where the teacher has her back to you. The clock, you notice, almost seems to have started going backwards.

You need excitement. Something, anything.

You fill a pipette with water, open the mysterious jar, and release a single drop. You just have time to think, "What's the worst that can happen?"

Then a vortex swallows Clare up, and she starts falling.

The last thing Clare sees is the clock on the wall, and this time there's no doubt. It's going backwards very fast indeed.

TIME-TRAVELLING CHEMISTRY, PART 1: FIRE

The scene: Earth, at the dawn of humanity.

With a thump, Clare lands on the savannah. She looks over the landscape of a pre-civilization world – the deep red of the soil, the dark brown of volcanic rock, the majestic shadow of a thorn tree in the sunset – and, quite sensibly, she feels a sense of profound terror.

Later, there will be some pretty serious questions that need answering. Such as: do they have lions 300,000 years ago?

But for now, before Clare ponders on how, midway through producing the finest spitball known to Year 10 Chemistry, she had somewhat unexpectedly time-travelled to the Stone Age, there is a more pressing matter.

To wit: what do you do about the large group of humans you've just spotted charging towards you?

The answer (and it's surprising, frankly, that you even had to ask) is dazzle them with your Chemistry skills.

Back here in deep time, our ancestors had yet to fully control the invention that would allow them to conquer the world. They had yet to master fire.

Sure, they could use it. They could capture

it from forest fires and they could keep the fires burning. They could even – perhaps – make it, with enough stick-rubbing. But they could not just produce it on demand, like striking a match.

But Clare is a modern human – and modern humans have mastered not just fire, but fireworks and iPads and aeroplanes. More than that, they have invented National Geographic survival shows.

So Clare knows just what to do to impress this ancient tribe – after all, she's seen it on TV.

She picks up two sticks, and starts rubbing vigorously.

One snaps.

If only she had a lighter…

As Clare thinks back to the survival programmes, she sees a flint axe glinting. On the ground she sees a rock doing the same.

Of course! She can make her own lighter.

When you turn the wheel on a lighter, steel strikes against flint, and little particles of the iron fly off. The friction is enough to heat them, until they ignite and make sparks.

The same trick was probably employed by some Stone Age humans to start their fires, except rather than steel they used iron pyrite – better known as fool's gold.

As luck would have it, that is just the rock by Clare's feet (if we are allowed to use time travel as a convenient plot device, we are certainly allowed to use geology).

As luck would also (sort of) have it, a flint axe is currently arcing towards her head.

Maybe these Stone Age folk aren't so friendly.

Clare dodges, she leaps, she grabs the axe and strikes it against the iron pyrite – making a shower of sparks, which flash in the dusk. There's an awed gasp.

While her distant ancestors look on, Clare takes the opportunity to pull together some kindling and – the producer of that National Geographic show would be so proud – bring humanity firmly into the age of fire.

CHAPTER 2

BONDING

INTRODUCTION
BONDING

IN THIS CHAPTER YOU WILL LEARN ABOUT:

- Ionic bonds
- Covalent bonds
- Metallic bonds
- Alloys

A world of just elements is a boring place.

There is nothing in us that is not an element, but we are so much more complex than that implies. Because it is only when elements combine with other elements – their atoms coming together – that the world gets interesting.

Join carbon with two oxygens, and you get the gas that keeps the world warm enough for life: carbon dioxide.

Join carbon with a few nitrogens, hydrogens and phosphorus, and you get the long twisty chemical that life uses to reproduce – better known as DNA.

Join carbon instead with a different proportion of hydrogen and oxygen, and you get a chemical that one sort of life – humans – uses to celebrate things: alcohol.

And that's just carbon.

This is a chapter about what happens when elements combine – and how, in doing so, the few dozen blocks that make up the universe produce an abundance of life, in all its complexity.

CRYSTALS

One day in 2000, two Mexican miners were digging a tunnel 300 m underground. Working in the intense heat, they suddenly and unexpectedly drilled into a cavern.

They swept their torches around into the blackness beyond, and wherever the light swept it reflected back – flashing off strange, angular surfaces.

Slowly, they adjusted their eyes to the new view and, methodically illuminating the cave, began to form a picture of what was inside.

After doing so, they rushed to the surface and told their boss he had to shut the tunnel, block the exit and reroute it.

Because they had just happened on a natural wonder of the world.

In that cave were by far the largest natural crystals ever found – great spears of gypsum, the size of trees.

1 m wide, 10 m tall, they formed a jagged jewel-scape, like the wonky teeth of a vast crocodile in desperate need of dentistry.

And the mining company realized it needed to preserve the cave for the world.

HOW DID THEY FORM?

Crystals are almost mind-bogglingly regular in their atomic structure.

This does not normally happen. Knowing how a single brick joins to another brick is not normally enough to tell you the structure that a billion of them make. Imagine if, just by looking at two Egyptian bricks, you could tell they would inevitably form the Great Pyramid of Giza.

The most astonishing thing about these huge crystals in that Mexican cave, is their shape can be almost entirely explained by the bonding behaviour of something a billion, billion, billion times smaller – the individual atoms.

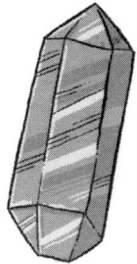

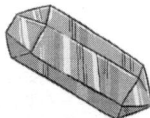

Under certain circumstances (for instance a hot cave filled with mineral-rich water), atoms can come together in set repeating patterns.

So far, so usual. Lots of things when locked together at the atomic level look nicely ordered. But what is amazing about crystals, is that they remain ordered, making a smooth geometric structure, even when you look at them at the non-atomic scale – using the weak eyes of a human.

In the case of the Mexican cave, the astonishing crystals had formed using a particular kind of bond, known as an ionic bond.

But it is probably best to explain that bond using a crystal you will be rather more familiar with: sodium chloride, better known as "salt".

IONIC BONDING

Remember how electron shells work? The first shell fills up with two electrons. If an element has more electrons it starts filling up the second shell until it has eight electrons. Then it moves onto the third.

Sodium is a metal with 11 electrons. That means its first two shells are full and its third has a single electron.

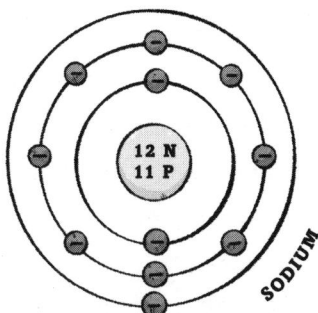

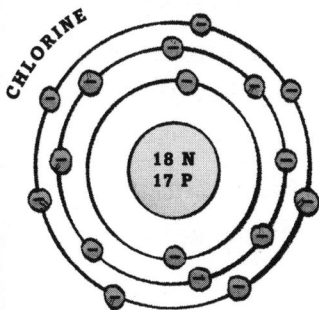

Chlorine is not a metal and has 17 electrons. That means its first shell is full, its second is full as well, while its third has seven electrons in – so is one short of being full.

When the two different elements react, they transfer electrons: they borrow from each other to make their shells full. The sodium atom transfers it outer shell electron to the outer shell of the chlorine atom: by doing this both atoms have now achieved full outer shells. This means, though, that they have a charge.

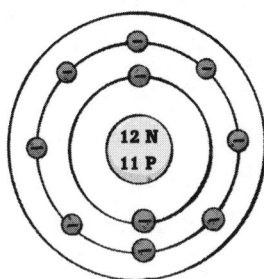

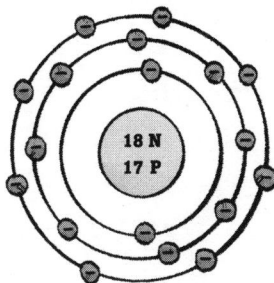

SODIUM   CHLORINE

Atoms don't normally have charges. The number of electrons matches the number of protons. But the sodium, which just lost one of its negative electrons is positive. The chlorine, which gained an electron, is negative.

They are "ions" – charged particles. And they attract each other, joining together in a lattice.

The extremely strong bonds of these ionic lattices mean crystals like this have several characteristic properties: a very high melting point, an extremely high boiling point and, in the case of sodium chloride, a structure that makes chips tasty.

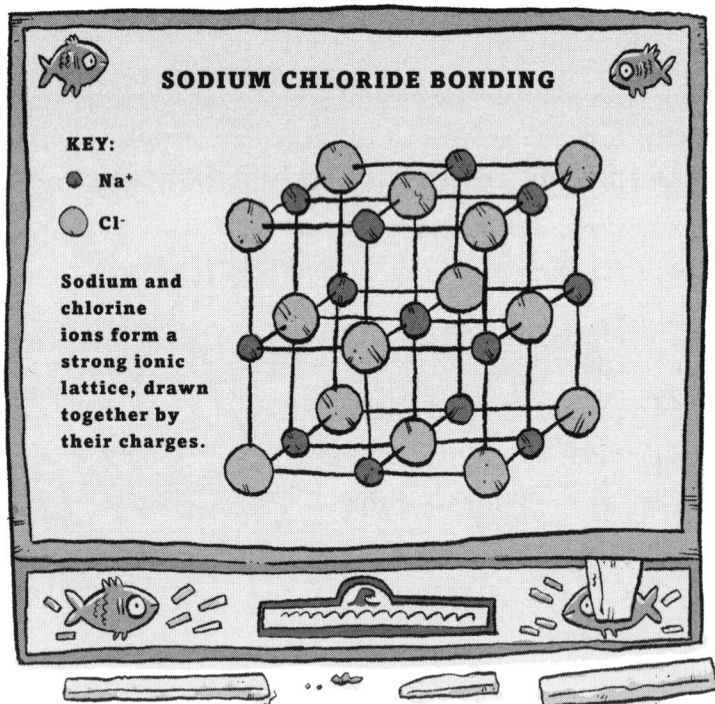

SODIUM CHLORIDE BONDING

KEY:

Na^+

Cl^-

Sodium and chlorine ions form a strong ionic lattice, drawn together by their charges.

This can be written as a word equation:

sodium + chlorine » sodium chloride

It can also be written as symbolic equation, using the symbols in the Periodic Table:

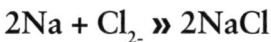

2Na + Cl$_2$ » 2NaCl

COVALENT BONDING

Sometimes, atoms don't borrow – they share.

Take ammonia, for instance, which is made from nitrogen and hydrogen.

Nitrogen has seven electrons, so two in its first shell and then five in its second, part-full, shell.

Hydrogen has one electron, in its half-full first shell.

It is harder to make an ion of nitrogen (although it does happen) – gaining three electrons is a fairly ambitious goal.

There is, though, another way of completing their shells. By sharing: by forming a "covalent" bond.

The nitrogen needs three extra electrons, and takes those from three hydrogens.

But at the same time the hydrogens need an electron each – and take those from the nitrogen.

The electrons are used twice, to complete each shell.

Sometimes, atoms covalently bond to their own kind, forming a compound containing only one type of atom.

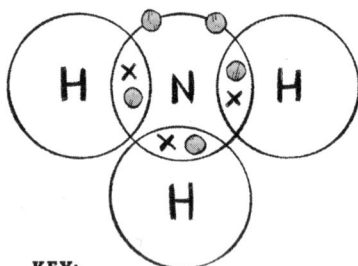

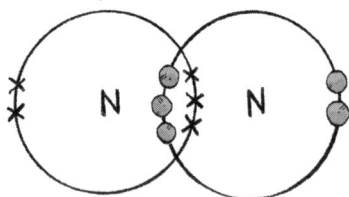

They each share three electrons, so that both has eight in their outer shell.

GIANT COVALENT MOLECULES: CARBON

The difference between a pencil "lead" and a diamond ring is a single covalent bond – and about a thousand pounds.

Nowhere is the importance of bonding clearer than when you contrast a black, cheap, soft substance that you have in your pencil case with the hardest natural object in existence.

Graphite and diamonds have two similarities, though. The first, is that they contain carbon and nothing else; the second, is that they are both examples of giant covalent bonds.

Unlike oxygen molecules, for instance, where two atoms join together to make a single structure (which is then free to float around untethered as a gas) in diamond and graphite, carbon atoms join into a bonded lattice. A lattice that can, in theory, continue indefinitely.

The easiest of the two bonds to understand – if not to get your hands on! – is diamond.

A diamond is a structure of carbon in which every carbon atom is joined to four more carbons, sharing an electron with each.

This structure has a lot of bonds, meaning it is very hard to tear the atoms apart. That's why diamond is strong and has a very high melting point.

And with no free electrons to move, as they're all tied up in bonds, there is no way to conduct electricity; so it's not all that useful.

Still … it does look pretty in a ring.

Graphite is a little different. It is bonded so that each carbon atom is only joined to three others, forming layers stacked on top of each other.

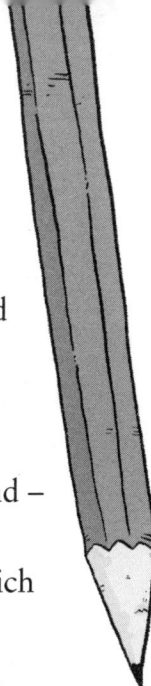

DIAMOND STRUCTURE

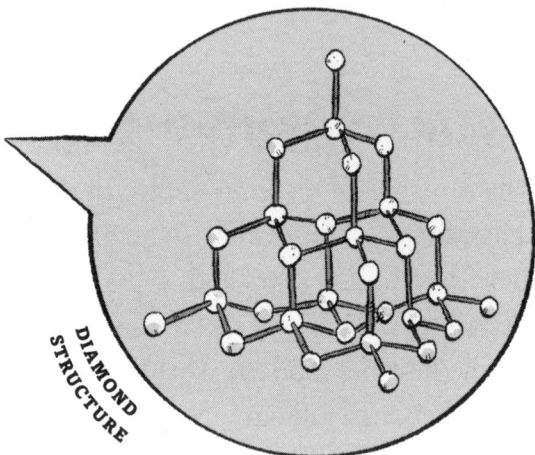

This means two things. The first is, it's less strong. With fewer bonds and no complete outer shells it's easier to smear onto, for instance, paper.

The second is that, with all those spare electrons bouncing around, it can conduct electricity.

GRAPHITE STRUCTURE

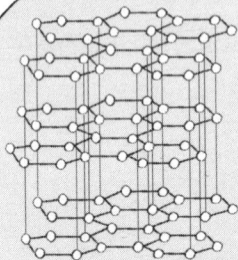

Atoms in one layer

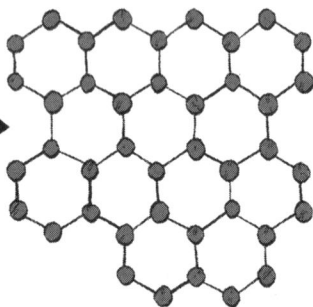

A stack of layers

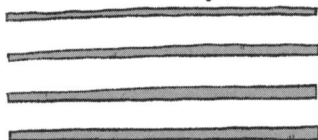

METALLIC BONDING

The Tollense River is an unremarkable waterway that cuts a shallow valley through north-eastern Germany. 3,200 years ago, 4,000 men met here for a terrible battle – and the river ran red with blood.

The first the modern world learnt of that battle was when, in 1996, an amateur archaeologist found an arm bone sticking out of the soil.

Today, the evidence of that battle is still being uncovered. There are bones that have been hacked and smashed, skulls with arrows embedded deep inside – the remains of hundreds of men.

It was clearly a desperate conflict, but little to nothing is known about it. These people living on the banks of a small German river were illiterate; their heroism unrecorded, their treachery lost from history.

So we cannot know who was fighting whom, or why. But we can see that this battle came at a transition point.

One arrow, lodged firmly in one arm, is flint. Another, found in a skull, is of a green tarnished metal. Some bones show the deep gashes of metal swords, yet their owners are holding wooden clubs.

Here is where the Stone Age met the Bronze Age – where a new kind of super-material was wielded on the European battlefield.

And the side that did not master it did not stand a chance.

WHY BRONZE?

We don't generally talk about Tin Ages or Copper Ages. Yet both of those are needed for the bronze used on that battlefield in Germany.

The reason we don't consider those metals worthy of an "age" would rapidly become apparent to anyone who tried to make a sword out of them.

Tin is so soft that you can bash it into the shape you want at room temperature.

Copper's great advantage today is that it is so soft it can be pulled into wires – useful for internet connections, but less useful for arrowheads.

Copper is most commonly found in wires

Pure metal of almost any kind is pretty soft. The reason why is the way it is bonded. Metal atoms are joined together neither covalently nor ionically.

Instead, the electrons in their last shell – which is unfilled – "delocalize". They free themselves from the nucleus, and join with those of all the other metal atoms.

These ions are held together by a soup of negatively-charged electrons.

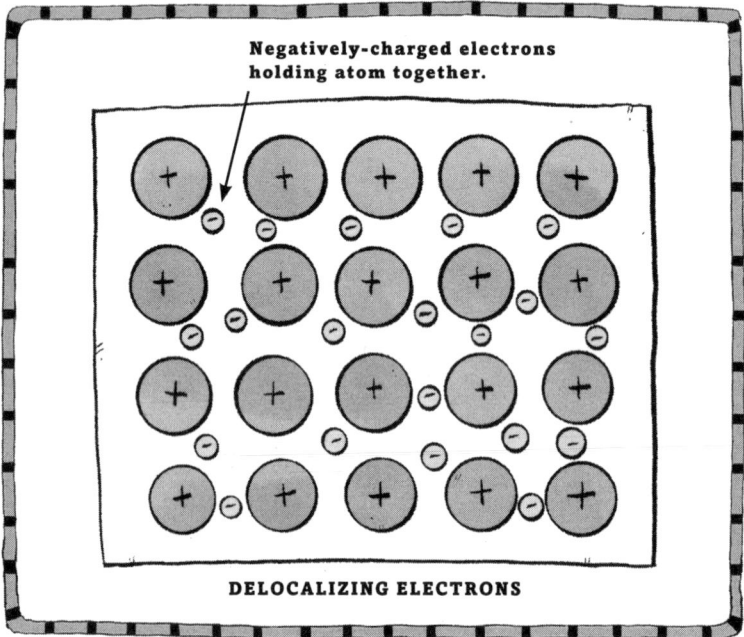

Negatively-charged electrons holding atom together.

DELOCALIZING ELECTRONS

All these free electrons mean metals are brilliant at conducting heat and electricity.

But this giant metallic structure, with lots of identical ions layered among electrons, also has a flaw. It is very easy to slide those layers over each other, which makes it far less effective at, say, shattering an enemy's skull.

This is why the invention of bronze was so incredible. When two soft metals – copper and a little bit of tin – came together, they formed something astonishing.

They formed a metal that built empires, vanquished enemies and changed humanity forever.

The fact that bronze is strong isn't just a fluke.

It is strong because alloys,

Tin (Sn) atoms get in the way of the uniform lattice of copper (Cu) atoms and stop them sliding

which is the word for metals mixed with other metals (or sometimes impurities such as carbon), of any kind are strong.

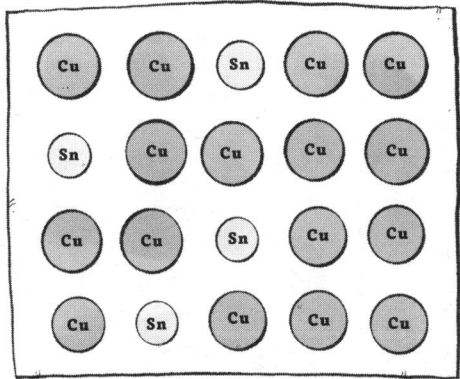

While in a pure metal the layers are free to slide over each other, in an alloy there are impurities from what it is mixed with. And these impurities act like a kind of grit.

The different-sized atoms stop the sliding, holding the layers in place.

And by stopping the atoms from sliding, alloys make a metal that can be used in tools, in ornaments that survive to this day ...

... and which, on that day beside the Tollense River, produced arrows that didn't stop until they reached the brain.

IN SHORT: Chemistry can be a bonding experience – if you know your ionic compounds from your covalent ones.

WHAT YOU NEED TO KNOW

- Metal atoms lose electrons to become positive ions. Non-metals gain electrons to become negative ions. They lose or gain an amount that means they have a full outer shell.
- An ionic compound is formed from a lattice of positive and negative ions, tightly bonded together, joined by their opposite charges.
- Covalent bonds form when atoms share electrons, again to make their outer shell full.
- Covalently-bonded atoms can form giant molecules, with the atoms bonded in endlessly-repeating patterns. These have strong intramolecular forces so they are hard to melt.
- Diamond and graphite are both made from covalently-bonded carbon, but the pattern of bonds gives the two substances very different properties.
- Metals are bonded differently. The electrons in their outer shell "delocalize", and hold together the nuclei in a soup of negative charge.
- Metals are typically soft, meaning they can be moulded.
- Alloys, in which a metal is mixed with another element, are often strong. The different-sized atoms of the other element stop layers of metal sliding over each other.

TIME-TRAVELLING CHEMISTRY, PART 2: CHARCOAL

It could have been worse, Clare thinks to herself.

Yes, she is no longer in double Chemistry. Yes, it is 300,000 years ago. But on the other hand, she is no longer in double Chemistry. And she is alive.

Rather than killing her, as Clare had feared, the tribe have taken her to their cave and now – impressed by her fire-making prowess – seem to be praising her.

Which is mildly awkward but, Clare likes to think, only reasonable. And it's definitely better than getting bashed on the head with a stone axe.

There is one small issue though: the smoke.

It is getting increasingly hard to see; her eyes are stinging and everyone is coughing. A fire at the mouth of an unventilated cave is not a great idea.

What she needs, she realizes, is a fuel that makes less smoke.

What she needs is charcoal.

Charcoal has been used by almost every civilization that has ever existed. It is wood, but without all the extras.

Wood burns because the carbon in it reacts with oxygen to make carbon dioxide. Wood is a complex substance though, containing carbon, water, hydrogen and lots of other things – ranging from organic polymers to dead bugs.

If you are looking to make heat, all you want from wood is the carbon. Everything else makes the smoke, soot and steam that get in your eyes.

So how do you get the carbon? The answer is through a process called *pyrolysis*, in which wood is heated in the near-absence of oxygen.

Clare rubs her eyes, then sets about creating the conditions for pyrolysis by making a circular woodpile.

There are many ways of making charcoal, but among the simplest is to pile up wood, set a small amount of it burning in the centre, then cover the whole pile with turf to restrict the oxygen.

If done right, the surrounding wood is very slowly burnt to make charcoal – leaving behind almost pure carbon.

When Clare tries out this pure carbon charcoal in the fire, she is satisfied to see it does indeed make a lot less smoke. It also burns a lot hotter, she notices, and that's when an idea begins to form.

Here, in this cave, she has the opportunity to advance humanity by hundreds of thousands of years. With science, she can give the species the knowledge to conquer the world.

Their descendants, she imagines, can build the pyramids, sail the seas and visit the Moon – and thanks to her help, they can achieve all that millennia earlier. With the right steer, they can reach technological heights and all before the humans in the timeline she left have developed the wheel.

And if that also means, Clare idly thinks, that she is honoured for ever more as the founding genius of humanity? Or perhaps, she daydreams further, a demigod?

Well, every selfless gesture deserves its compensations. It is time to introduce this tribe to some Stone Age Chemistry.

CHAPTER 3

QUANTITATIVE CHEMISTRY

INTRODUCTION
QUANTITATIVE CHEMISTRY

IN THIS CHAPTER YOU WILL LEARN ABOUT:

- Avogadro's constant
- The mole
- Relative formula mass
- Avogadro's law

You can't see Chemistry. When two hydrogen atoms join with an oxygen one, we know they make water – but we never see what that molecule looks like.

This is odd. Studying Chemistry is like studying literature without being able to read individual words, or becoming an expert on sailing without ever stepping into a boat.

To make the subject work, to turn it into a proper science, chemists need to be able to count the atoms themselves.

They need to find a way to relate the unimaginably small – the individual molecules in water, for instance – to something we can see: an ice cube, or a glass of water.

This chapter is about how they do it, using some very big numbers to describe some very small things.

THE KILOGRAM AND THE AVOGADRO SPHERE

For 130 years, the kilogram lived in a vault in Paris.

Note: not *a* kilogram, but *the* kilogram.

Kept underground, behind a steel door whose lock required three keys – only one of which was kept in France – this was the single object that defined mass for the entire world.

Before 2019, if you stood on the scales in your bathroom and the reading said "60.2 kg", what that meant is you weighed the same as 60.2 of those Parisian metal lumps.

If you bought a 500 g bag of sugar, it was half a Parisian lump.

But, in the late twentieth century, scientists began to realize there was a problem with the kilogram.

It was, they suspected, losing weight.

Worse: that was, by definition, impossible.

That Parisian lump had to always and unchangingly be a kilogram. If, somehow, a careless cleaner rubbed it so vigorously it lost half its metal, it would still weigh a kilogram – simply because it could be nothing else. The kilogram is, by definition, it.

The mass loss wasn't much, in case you are worried. If an ant walked across the kilogram it would have cancelled out the effect 100 times over.

But this was still a real annoyance.

They needed a solution – a better definition of a kilogram. A definition that did not mean the whole world relied on one lump of metal to define mass.

They needed to define it, instead, in terms of something unchanging: a definition so fundamental that you could explain it to an alien, and they would instantly understand what a kilogram was.

They came up with not one solution, but two.

The first solution involved using a piece of weighing equipment so sensitive that you needed to know the position of the moon before you used it; otherwise, its gravitational pull would interfere.

The second they came up with – the one we are talking about here – involved a shimmering, mesmerizing ball, 9.4 cm in diameter, of pure silicon: the Avogadro sphere.

To understand how it worked though, you need to first understand some of the most important concepts in Chemistry.

RELATIVE ATOMIC MASS

Remember atomic mass from Chapter One?

Rather than perform calculations using the real mass of an atom, with all of the long strings of decimals that involves, you learnt a way to convert the mass to something manageable – by just relating the atoms to each other.

So carbon is 12, hydrogen is 1 and oxygen, which is one and a third times as heavy as carbon, is 16.

The principle works for compounds too. A molecule of carbon dioxide, CO_2, has a "relative formula mass" of 44 (12 for the carbon, and 2 x 16 for the oxygen).

CARBON DIOXIDE

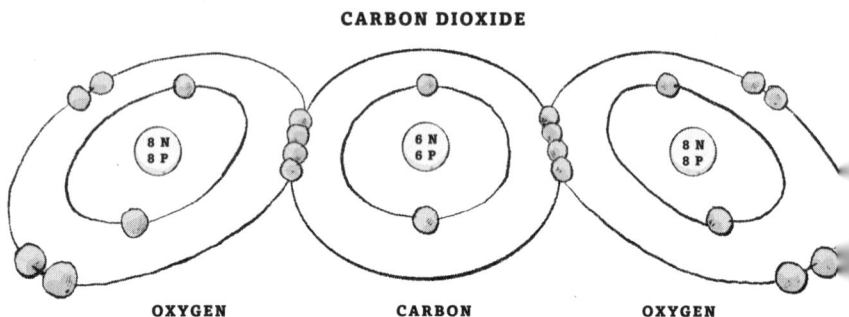

OXYGEN · · · · · · · · · · · CARBON · · · · · · · · · · · OXYGEN

The problem with relative atomic mass is, of course, it doesn't relate it to our own, non-atomic world. It is just a number.

Yet there is a clever way to bring it back to our world, and still keep things simple.

THE MOLE

To the great sadness of Chemistry students, the mole is not named after burrowing animals – but molecules. It is a measure of "amount", or number of things.

You can have a mole of potassium atoms, a mole of carbon atoms, or a mole of moles (the burrowing animals). In all cases, what that means is you have 6.02×10^{23} of them. Or, if you prefer, 602,000,000,000,000,000,000,000 – a number known as **Avogadro's constant.**

A mole of potassium is 602 thousand billion billion atoms. A mole of moles is 602 thousand billion billion burrowing creatures.

Here is the clever bit. This number is not chosen at random. It is chosen to ensure that calculations involving moles get a lot simpler.

If the atomic mass of an atom is 4, then a mole of it (the "it" being, in this case, helium) weighs 4 g.

Carbon has an atomic mass of 12, so a mole of it weighs 12 g.

The uranium in an atomic bomb has an atomic mass of 235, so a mole weighs 235 g.

Or, put another way, 602 thousand billion billion helium atoms weigh 4 g, that many carbon atoms weigh 12 g and that many uranium atoms weigh 235 g.

A mole, meanwhile, weighs about 90 g. So a mole of moles is roughly the mass of the Moon.

All right then, so in a purely practical sense, you probably can't have a mole of moles.

Or, rather, you can numerically – but if you did they would definitely play merry havoc on the neighbours' lawn.

AVOGADRO'S CONSTANT

The number 6.02×10^{23} is very big indeed.

(As anyone who has tried to collect together that many moles would be able to confirm.)

Avogadro's constant is named after a nineteenth-century Italian chemist, Amedeo Avogadro, who spent a lot of time thinking about the relationship between the number of particles of a substance and how much space – and mass – they take up.

> Avogadro's constant is a way of calculating the number of particles in a known mass of a substance.

When we breathe in oxygen, we do not breathe in single atoms, but molecules: two oxygen atoms joined together, each of which has an atomic mass of 16.

This means that the "**relative formula mass**" of an oxygen molecule is 32, as that is **16 + 16**.

If we have 32 g of oxygen molecules then we have one mole – and so we have $\mathbf{6.02 \times 10^{23}}$ molecules.

If we have 64 g, we have two moles – $\mathbf{12.04 \times 10^{23}}$.

In this way, you can use the mass of something to say how many atoms or molecules are in it.

> **Amount in moles = mass of substance /relative formula mass**

> **Particles = amount in moles x Avogadro's constant.**

So, for instance, imagine you have 27 g of water. Water has a formula mass of **18 (H_2O = 2x1 + 16)**. This means that 18 g would be one mole, so 27 g is 1.5 moles. If one mole of water has **6.02 x 10^{23}** molecules, 1.5 moles has 50 per cent more – or **9.03 x 10^{23}**.

Now here's the really, really clever bit; the trick the Avogadro sphere relies on when it redefines the kilogram: the formula does not have to work that way round.

If you know the mass, you can calculate how many particles there are – which means if you know how many particles there are, you can reverse it and calculate mass.

Obviously to do that, you would have to count the number of particles, which would be ridiculous...

AVOGADRO'S SPHERE

The Avogadro sphere is the smoothest object on the planet. If the Earth were as smooth, the height difference between the deepest ocean and the tallest mountain would be just 5 m.

It is so smooth that you cannot see it spin – there is no blemish or undulation for your eye to catch on.

The reason why it was made this way is that, when it was constructed, the scientists needed to know its volume precisely; to the nearest particle, in fact. Because, they intended to count them.

The sphere is a single crystal of silicon-28, machined to be exactly the same mass as the Parisian kilogram.

From it, scientists worked out how many atoms of silicon made up a kilogram – meaning that they also had an estimate, to the greatest precision ever, of Avogadro's constant.

Now having done that, it is possible to do the reverse.

A kilogram, today, is no longer defined with reference to a changeable lump of metal in a vault in Paris. It can be defined by using a precise number of silicon atoms.

Around 21,525,387,297,294 million, million, in case you're wondering.

AVOGADRO'S LAW

Avogadro doesn't just have a number and a sphere. Avogadro has a law, too.

There are several ways of describing Avogadro's law. Here is a way that Amedeo Avogadro – Italian nobleman, distinguished chemist, originator of everything Avogadro – would not have used.

Imagine that you blow up a balloon using your lungs. Imagine that you blow up another balloon to the same size using a helium canister. Imagine that you blow up a third identical balloon, to exactly the same size as the first two, using the methane from your bottom.

Even as you watch the helium balloon disappear into the sky, even as you wonder what would happen were you to pop the one filled with methane, there is a fact even more incredible than the stench that would produce.

Each balloon, with each of its wildly different gases, has exactly the same number of molecules.

At the same pressure and the same temperature, Avogadro argued that any fixed volume of gas – whether helium, methane, or nitrogen (along with the other gases that come out of your lungs or bottom) – has the same number of particles in it.

So whether you blow up a balloon with your lungs or your bottom, the same amount of gas molecules bounce around inside.

It turned out, incredibly, that he was right: what matters in a gas is not the type of particle but the number. And the world's chemists were so impressed that they named a constant after him.

IN SHORT: You'll never look at farting into a balloon in the same light again.

WHAT YOU NEED TO KNOW:

- The mole is a measure of "amount".
- A mole of an element weighs its relative atomic mass in grams. So a mole of carbon-12 weighs 12 g.
- In one mole there are 6.02×10^{23} atoms or molecules. That number is known as Avogadro's constant.
- Any volume of gas at a fixed temperature and pressure has the same number of molecules in it.
- A mole of a gas occupies a volume of 22.4 litres, at room temperature and pressure.

TIME-TRAVELLING CHEMISTRY, PART 3: POTTERY

If Clare knew that she was drinking from a vessel made from dried animal skin, she reckons she could probably come round to the idea.

Even if she knew it was made from a definite organ (maybe a wild boar's bladder, say) then she would probably be able to drink with only the minimum amount of retching.

But when she pointed at the floppy "bottle" they are all drinking from and mimed to ask what it was made from, all that the tribesperson did was point vaguely to her stomach.

This was not comforting.

Worse, her reticence – a polite word for utter disgust – at putting her lips to the bottle is not just causing dehydration. It is also causing offence.

She is no longer as popular as she once was.

It is time, Clare thinks, to teach the tribe how to make pottery. It is time to make a watertight drinking vessel that does not originate in an undefined part of an undefined animal.

The first step is to find clay. Luckily, it is everywhere; clay is a particular collection of minerals, often found in riverbeds, that come from weathered rocks.

What is great about clay, is that when it is wet it is "plastic" – not plastic in the sense of the material that you make Lego out of, but plastic in the sense that it is mouldable.

So, you can make it into a shape, and it stays in that shape.

The reason clay has this property, is that it forms in layers, with the layers joined to each other using a thin film of water molecules. The water molecules are enough to hold the clay in place, just not very strongly.

This means you can still move the clay. When you do, the layers slide past each other, but when you stop the water holds it together again.

Which means, in turn, that it can be made it into the shape of a cup.

All well and good, but really, Clare feels, she needs something a bit more solid – something at least as effective as a floppy bladder-type thing.

This is where pottery, and Chemistry, comes in.

First, wiping the sweat from her forehead, she dries the clay in the sun.

Then, things get even hotter. With the charcoal, and a bit more earth moving, Clare knows she now has the ability to make a kiln that will reach 1000 degrees Celsius or more.

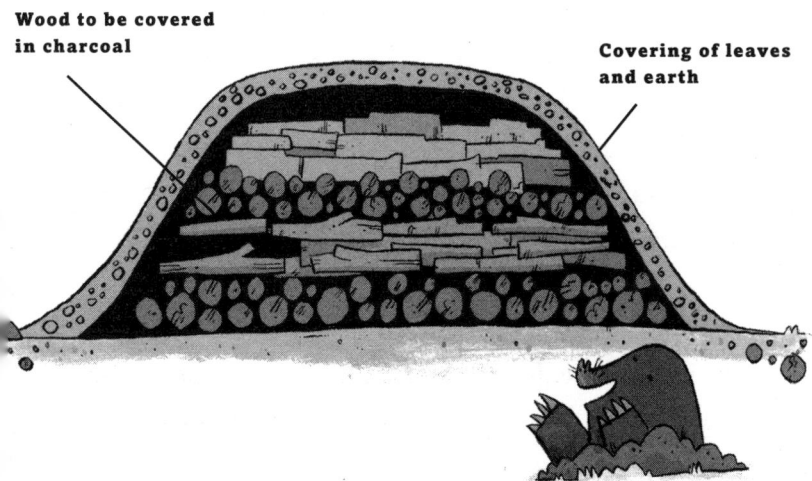

Wood to be covered in charcoal

Covering of leaves and earth

At 500 degrees Celsius, changes start to happen in the clay. The water inside that held it together is chemically removed. In the process, what were once weak hydrogen bonds become strong oxygen ones.

Then, as the temperature increases further, the minerals themselves start to melt.

They "vitrify", forming a glassy "glue" that holds it together. And it becomes terracotta – which means "cooked earth" in Italian. (Panna cotta, in case you are wondering about the dessert, means "cooked cream").

Clare wants it to be completely watertight, so there is one more step. She coats the inside in wood ash, puts it back in the kiln, and watches as the minerals in the ash help form a glaze.

And as she watches it cool, as the tribespeople tentatively tap the outside of a large pot, Clare congratulates herself. Technology-wise, she has just advanced humanity by 250,000 years.

CHAPTER 4

ACIDS, ALKALIS AND SALTS

INTRODUCTION
ACIDS, ALKALIS AND SALTS

IN THIS CHAPTER YOU WILL LEARN ABOUT:

- The definition of an acid
- The definition of an alkali
- How they react
- The scale used to measure them

When chemists appear in films, generally cackling with wild hair in front of mysterious bubbling flasks, there will normally be an acid involved in their concoction at some point.

You can see why. Acids are the terrible liquids used to burn through bank vaults, to dispose of bodies and (on occasion) to threaten captured super spies, unless they talk.

There is a flaw – albeit a slightly boring one – in this view of acids. Of course there will be one bubbling in the flask, for the simple reason that almost all liquids are either acids, or their equally corrosive opposite, alkalis.

The slight difference is, few will be much threat to a super spy. Even tap water is an acid.

This is a chapter about acids, which are liquids with roaming hydrogen ions, and alkalis, which are liquids with roaming hydroxide ions.

It is about what we do with them, what they do with other chemicals and – because, as film directors know, the strong ones are the most fun – what happens when we use them to dissolve things.

ACIDS

It was 1940. The Nazis had arrived on the streets of Copenhagen in Denmark, and George de Hevesy realized he was responsible for the lives of two men.

If they were to live, he had to find a way to hide two big lumps of gold.

When war had looked likely, two German scientists – one Jewish, and another who sympathized with the Jews – had sent George and his boss, the scientist Niels Bohr, their Nobel Prizes for safe keeping.

Both feared that the Nazi state would take the prizes from them otherwise.

But now war had indeed come, and it had spread farther than they had feared.

GEORGE
DE HEVESY

Worse, on the gold Nobel medallions were engraved the names of the two scientists: Max von Laue and James Franck.

If the Nazis found the medals, they would know who had sent them, and that they had broken laws against exporting gold.

They would be executed. So, quite possibly, would George. He had to do something, and do it fast. But what?

George needed to think quickly, to be resourceful and to use all his ingenuity.

He needed Chemistry.

Quickly, he went into his laboratory and pulled down a bottle of aqua regia. Gold does not react with much – that's why it's so precious. But it does react with aqua regia, a mixture of hydrochloric and nitric acid.

The two acids work as a team. Neither will dissolve gold on its own, but together they have the skills.

First, the nitric acid rips some electrons off the surface of the medallion. That provides all the opening the hydrochloric acid needs – its negatively-charged chloride ions react with these now positively-charged gold atoms, to form a new molecule that dissolves to make a brown liquid.

And that was what the Nazis saw when they came to his laboratory. There on the shelf were a couple of boring bottles filled with a murky brown liquid.

Those bottles would sit there throughout the long occupation, unnoticed.

Then, when the war ended, George reversed the process. He extracted the gold, sent it to the Nobel committee, and the medals were recast.

The Nazis had been outfoxed by Chemistry.

NOBEL PRIZE

HOW DOES ACID WORK?

A Nobel Prize is not the most valuable object to succumb to acid. That accolade goes to Cleopatra's pearl.

One day, Cleopatra, the Queen of Egypt, promised to host the most expensive banquet in history.

Dish after dish arrived, of the finest produce the country could offer. But her guests were still not impressed.

It was a lavish meal, no doubt – but no more so than would be expected of a Queen.

Then, at the end, she took out her pearl earrings, the largest known to the ancient world, and popped them into a glass of vinegar.

Pearls might be valued as among the most exquisite objects produced by nature but, however expensive they are, they cannot break the laws of Chemistry.

The guests watched aghast as they, like the gold medals, dissolved in the acidic vinegar.

Why is it that acid will turn so many things to sludge? The answer is hydrogen.

Take hydrochloric acid. Its formula is HCl – one hydrogen atom with one chlorine atom. When it is dissolved in a strong solution with water, the H and the Cl split apart into ions.

The H is positive, having lost an electron, and the Cl is negative. This H+ ion is really attractive to other molecules and atoms, to the point where it acts like a chemical battering ram.

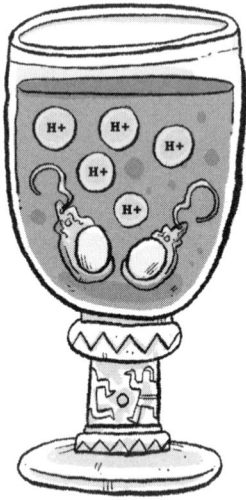

It bashes around, breaking up bonds and running rampant through compounds – tearing them apart and combining with their atoms.

The result is that if an acid is strong enough, almost nothing is safe. And if something is as delicate as a pearl, then even vinegar will do it.

So the story goes, after all the pearl had disappeared, Cleopatra looked across the heaving piles of food at her shocked guests. Then she glugged down the vinegar – making it indeed the most expensive banquet in history.

ALKALIS

Not long before Cleopatra was planning her party, on the other side of the Mediterranean, the Roman general Sertorius was also applying Chemistry to achieve his goals.

He had been sent to conquer some of the more defiant tribes on the fringes of the Roman Empire.

But he was dismayed to find that his enemy, the Characitani of Portugal, had selfishly decided *not* to meet him in the open to be slaughtered. Instead, they had ungallantly taken refuge in caves.

Never fear – he had Chemistry on his side. Unlike Cleopatra, he decided not to use acids but their opposite: **alkalis**.

Instead of **H+ ions**, alkalis have **OH- ions** – and they can be just as much of a menace to other compounds. They can also be easier to come by.

Quicklime is a powder, made from crushed and heated limestone, that forms an extremely strong alkali in water.

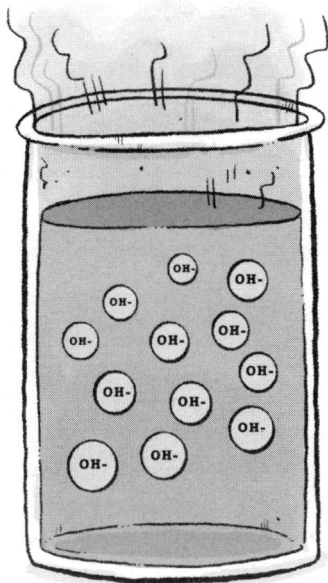

It is sometimes used during war or plague, when mass graves fill up and there is a risk of disease. Then, it is sprinkled on the bodies to lessen the smell.

As Sertorius realized though, it is useful not only in disposing of the dead, but in dealing with the living too.

He ground up quicklime powder and let the wind blow it into the caves – burning the Characitani's eyes and lungs.

They surrendered and Sertorius, rejoicing in the agonized cries of the Characitani, congratulated himself on another satisfactory conclusion to his military expeditions.

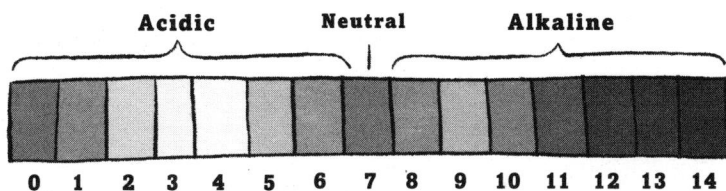

Acidic   **Neutral**   **Alkaline**

0   1   2   3   4   5   6   7   8   9   10   11   12   13   14

pH SCALE

The concentration of an acid or alkali is defined on the "**pH**" scale, which is a measure of how many H+ ions there are. What "pH " stands for is disputed. It may be "potential of hydrogen" or perhaps "power" or "potency".

When something is dissolved in water, there are always H+ ions and there are always OH- ions, but more H+ than OH- means that solution is acidic, while the reverse means it is alkaline.

The scale, which goes from 0 to 14, is **logarithmic** – which is a complicated word but a simple idea. It means that with each increase by 1, the H+ concentration decreases by a factor of ten.

A pH of 1 means it is an extremely strong acid, and there are lots of H+ ions. A pH of 13 means it is an extremely strong alkali, and there are very few H+ ions – and a lot of OH- ones.

And if you mix a ferociously-strong pH 1 acid with a ferociously-strong pH 13 alkali, all those angry OH- and H+ ions come together and produce something not ferocious at all: water.

ACIDS AND BASES, ACIDS AND METALS

There are two types of acid reaction you need to know about.

The first is what happened to Saint Peter's face. The second is what happened to Ulysses S. Grant's horse.

For centuries, Saint Peter has boldly looked out from the front of York Minster, the grand gothic cathedral in the centre of the city. Ever since the Middle Ages, his statue has bravely weathered wind, rain, hail and snow.

But in recent decades – in particular, towards the end of the twentieth century – the weather of Yorkshire took a turn for the worse.

With the effects of pollution, the rain started to become more acidic. And, slowly, Saint Peter's face dissolved away.

According to the Bible, Saint Peter was given his name by Jesus. Peter means rock and, said Jesus, "Upon this rock I will build my church; and the gates of Hades will not overpower it."

Perhaps he should have been a bit more specific about the rock he had in mind. Because this particular Peter, the York one, is made out of a rock called limestone – which, chemically-

speaking, is largely calcium carbonate ($CaCO_3$).

And whether or not Hades can overpower calcium carbonate, acid can.

ACID + BASE REACTION

Metal ions can join with oxide (O_{2-}), hydroxide (OH-) or carbonate (CO_3^{2-}) ions. The products of these unions are called **bases**.

Copper oxide, CuO, is a base. So, too, is sodium hydroxide, NaOH.

And so is calcium carbonate, $CaCO_3$.

When a base meets an acid, it reacts to form water and what is called a **salt**.

Acid + base » salt + water

WHAT IS A SALT?

Salts are what are left over when an acid reacts with a base and is "neutralized" – the OH- and H+ ions cancelling each other out. Initially, the salt will be dissolved in water, but if you evaporate it you end up with salt crystals.

There are lots of kinds of salt, but the one we know best is a salt of sodium and chloride – which is such a common salt, we just call it "salt".

For instance,

Sulphuric acid (H_2SO_4) + copper oxide (CuO) **»**
copper sulphate ($CuSO_4$) + water (H2O)

And (a slightly more complicated reaction):

Acid rain (HNO_3, nitric acid) + Saint Peter's face
($CaCO_3$) **»** melty crumbly face, otherwise known as
calcium nitrate: $Ca(NO_3)_2$ + water (H_2O) + carbon
dioxide (CO_2)*

* *When a carbonate is involved, you get carbon dioxide as well as water.*

What this means, in statue terms, is that York Minster recently had to commission a new Saint Peter, so that he can once again face the weather of Yorkshire with dignity.

For another few centuries, at least.

ULYSSES S. GRANT AND HIS HORSE

Ulysses S. Grant was one of the finest generals of the North in the American Civil War, and one of the worst presidents.

Such was his success on the battlefield that he became known as "Unconditional Surrender Grant" – because when opposing armies tried to attack him, that's what they ended up doing.

Naturally then, once the war was over, he had his own statue erected in Washington. Unlike Saint Peter, it was built to last: cast from bronze, which is mainly copper.

When, in peacetime, he was elected as President, he found that ruling was harder than crushing. One after another, officials in his government were accused of dishonesty, of bribe-taking, of tax avoidance.

This man, who could hold out against the full might of the slave-owning southern states, found it far more difficult to hold out against the insidious effects of corruption. Which was ironic ... because the same proved true of his statue.

Slowly, over the decades, this proud and noble general found that his horse became less and less handsome. Streaks of unsightly green appeared on its flank.

His steed, like Saint Peter, was succumbing to acid rain.

ACID + METAL REACTION

When acids meet metals, there is a different kind of reaction.

The simplest sort is this:

> **Acid + metal » salt + hydrogen**

So, for instance:

> **Sulphuric acid (H_2SO_4) + Magnesium (Mg) »**
> **Magnesium sulphate ($MgSO_4$) + Hydrogen (H_2)**

Some metals will react easily with acids. You can put them in a dilute acid and they start fizzing immediately, producing a continuous stream of little hydrogen bubbles.

Some, such as potassium, are so reactive that if you put them in water they violently flame up – making a metal hydroxide and hydrogen. That's why no one makes statues out of potassium.

THE REACTIVITY SERIES

The most reactive metals are those that lose electrons the most easily, to make positive ions. The least reactive, such as gold, find that difficult.

These are the metals, from most to least reactive:

1.	Potassium	9.	Nickel
2.	Sodium	10.	Tin
3.	Lithium	11.	Lead
4.	Calcium	12.	Copper
5.	Magnesium	13.	Mercury
6.	Aluminium	14.	Silver
7.	Zinc	15.	Gold
8.	Iron	16.	Platinum

People do make statues out of copper, though – and you can see why. It's almost as unreactive as silver and gold, but a lot cheaper (and unlike mercury, it has the benefit – when it comes to sculpting – of not being liquid).

Given enough time, and acidic-enough rain, even copper reacts eventually … as Grant's steed learnt to its cost.

This reaction is a bit more complicated, and

involves oxygen, carbon dioxide and acidic rain that come together to give Grant's steed a less shiny, and rather more green, sheen.

Luckily, US authorities have decided to intervene to protect the honour of their finest general.

Every couple of years, the noble and fearsome Ulysses S. Grant gets a gentle rub down from conservators, who smear a thin layer of wax over him to keep the elements off.

So these days, "Unconditional Surrender" Grant moisturizes.

IN SHORT: Don't buy jewellery for Cleopatra.

WHAT YOU NEED TO KNOW

- Acids make hydrogen ions when in water.
- Alkalis make hydroxide ions.
- They are both measured on the pH scale, which goes from 0 to 14.
- Anything with a pH less than 7 is acidic, and has more hydrogen ions than hydroxide. Anything more than 7 is alkaline.
- An acid mixed with a base – which is a hydroxide, oxide or carbonate – makes a salt and water (and carbon dioxide too, if it's a carbonate).
- An acid mixed with some metals will make a salt and hydrogen.

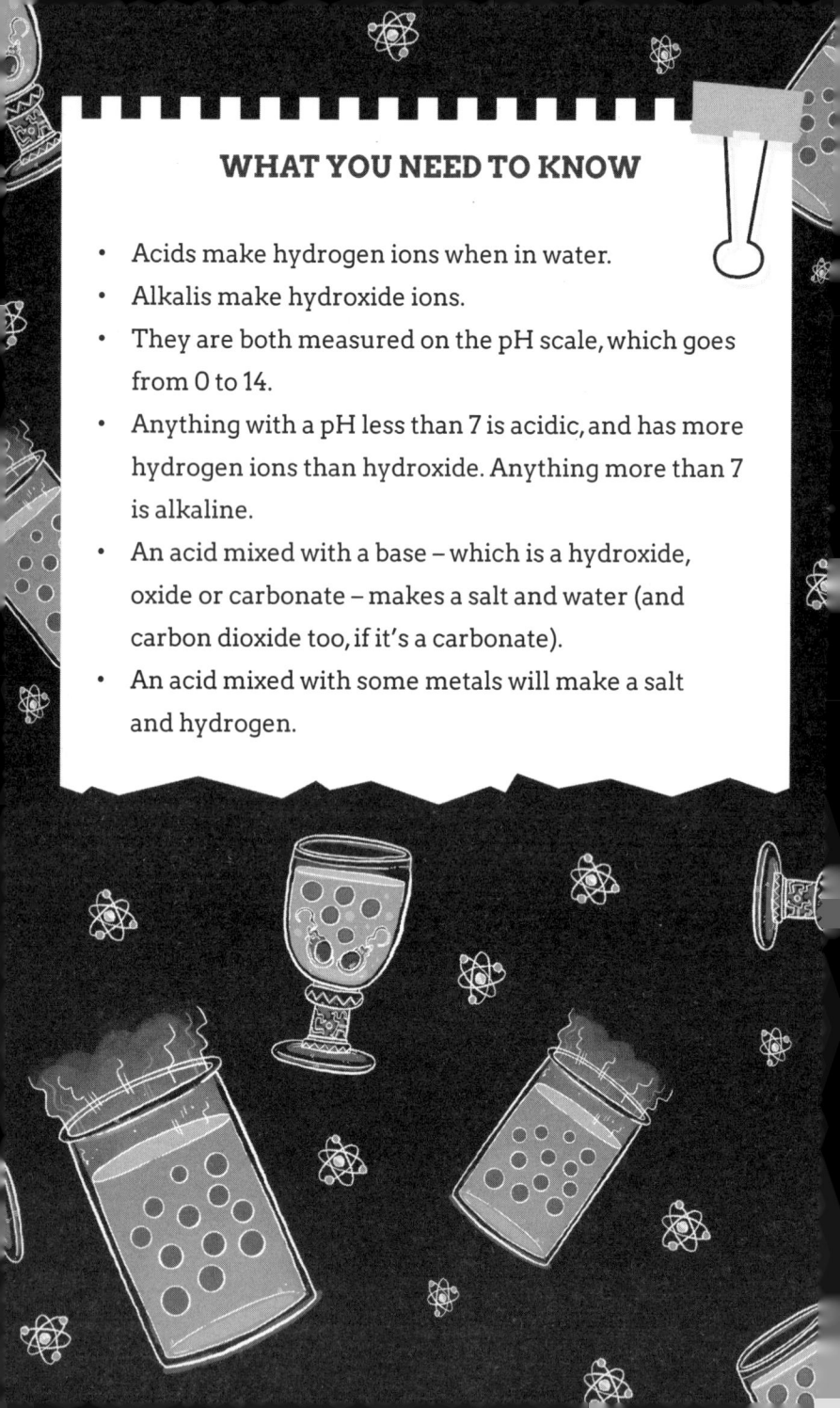

TIME-TRAVELLING CHEMISTRY, PART 4: SOAP

There is no getting around it, Clare thinks. She's starting to develop a certain aura: a whiff, an aroma … a *je ne sais quoi*.

If, as she is increasingly fearing, this is her home for good – that no vortex is ever going to return her to the delights of double Chemistry – then this needs to change.

What she needs is a good wash; what she needs is soap.

To know how soap works, it is important to understand how dirt works. The reason most things, including humans, get dirty is that they are oily.

The oil in our skin, for instance, combines with mud and is very hard to get off. The problem with oil is that it doesn't like water. It is "hydrophobic" – it repels water, and the two won't mix.

That is why long-distance swimmers grease themselves: the oily grease is a barrier between their warm bodies and the cold water.

That is also why water on its own won't clean greasy plates, or greasy humans.

This is where soap comes in; soap is something that brings oil and water together.

One end of a soap molecule is, like grease, hydrophobic. It is a long oily hydrocarbon, and will happily join to oil.

The other end is hydrophilic – it is charged and will join to water. So the molecule acts like a link, bringing these two hostile substances together and allowing the water to wash off the oil.

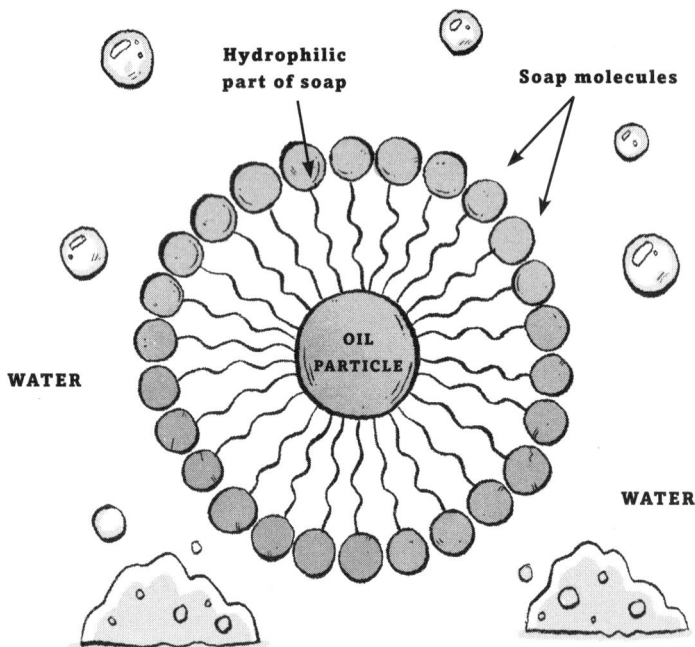

Hydrophilic part of soap

Soap molecules

OIL PARTICLE

WATER

WATER

How do you make such a magic molecule if you lived in the Stone Age? Well – and now might be time for fans of delicately-scented bath cubes to look away – the answer is with animal fat.

Soap is the salt of a fatty acid: it is what happens when you mix an alkali with the fat.

Now fat is no problem for Clare; that comes from animals.

Alkalis, it turns out, are not that hard either. That comes from what she and the Stone Age folk are cooking their animals in, from the same ash she used for glazing her pots.

Ash is the stuff in wood that doesn't burn. It is compounds of different minerals. The compounds Clare is interested in for her soap are the ones that dissolve in water.

To make an alkali – in this case one called potash – she has to put some wood ash in a pot, skim off anything floating, and then pour the water into another shallow pot to leave behind anything that is still undissolved.

When she lets that solution evaporate away, she is left with her compound.

All she has to do now is mix it with boiling animal fat and make humanity's first soap – albeit not one of the gently-scented variety.

At last, everyone can wash.

Later, though, it will be about far more than basic cleanliness.

One day, soap will be about life and death. The ability to wash, to really wash, is what means humans can live in their hundreds of thousands beside each other.

It was our first weapon against disease – and remains so in the twenty-first century.

But, today, Clare is just grateful for the smell.

Or, rather, that for the first time since she arrived here there isn't one.

CHAPTER 5

REACTIONS

INTRODUCTION
REACTIONS

IN THIS CHAPTER YOU WILL LEARN ABOUT:

- Exothermic reactions
- Endothermic reactions
- Activation energy
- Catalysts and reaction speed
- Reversible reactions

The most important substance involved in a chemical reaction is not even a chemical.

In a reaction, elements come together into **compounds**, and compounds switch into other compounds.

They make and break the bonds joining them to produce all the variety of chemicals we see in the world.

But all this is irrelevant without one substance, the single most important substance in the universe.

It is this precious substance that a lion is ultimately looking for when it tries to sink its teeth into a gazelle, and that a gazelle is relying on to escape those teeth.

It is the substance that gives the molecule **DNA** meaning, and the creatures that contain it, life.

That substance? **Energy**.

This chapter is about reactions that release energy, and those that consume it.

It is about how you get reactions started, how you speed them up and how – occasionally – they go in the other direction.

EXOTHERMIC REACTIONS

The Australian brush-turkey is 70 cm long and flightless.

It's crucial to the ecosystem of the Australian bush – helping to recycle the dead plant matter that provides nutrients on the forest floor.

It's also extremely annoying to have in your garden when it's feeling frisky. And that's because, while most birds build nests, very few build nests the size of a car.

In mating season, a male brush-turkey gathers tonnes of twigs and leaves, and puts them in a big mound. Extremely big; it's astonishing when encountered in the bush, and even more so when

encountered in a Sydney backyard.

It rakes up plant matter so fast that you can leave for work one morning with a pristine lawn and return at the end of the day, to find it replaced entirely with compost – and guarded by a bird, acting like it owns the place.

(Which, given the conservation laws for protecting Australian native animals, it sort of does.)

Upon being confronted with a steaming pile of compost, patrolled by a very angry turkey, Australian householders might reasonably question quite why it needed a nest that big.

The clue is in the word "steaming".

WHAT'S MAKING IT STEAM?

Most birds keep their eggs warm by sitting on them, using the heat of their body to ensure the egg does not get too cold.

But doing so is tedious, time-consuming – and means they are vulnerable to predators.

So the brush-turkeys don't bother. When they build their nests, they take advantage of what are called **exothermic reactions**.

From the moment the plant matter that the birds use to make their nests dies, microbes begin to break it down – and it becomes compost.

This plant matter contains lots of elements bonded together. Breaking bonds takes energy; making bonds releases some of that energy.

Some of that energy is used to make new bonds. But crucially, the energy needed to break old bonds is less than the energy released from the new ones... So, the excess energy is released as heat.

As it happens, this heat keeps the nest of the brush-turkey steaming along at around 33 degrees Celsius: just the temperature needed to incubate brush-turkey eggs.

If a female comes along and lays her eggs in that nest then, provided the male left enough plant matter, they will be incubated without any need for a bird's bottom.

Terence the Turkey wakes up and feels a bit different. There are tinglings, stirrings. Romance is in the air. Terence needs to find his Theresa.

As all romantic brush-turkeys know, to win a fair lady you need compost. Terence makes a pile of dead plants – which store energy in their chemical bonds.

In the compost pile, microbes begin to break down the bonds – providing the activation energy for a reaction.

Outside the compost pile, like a chivalrous knight of old, our hero deals with any angry Australians who inexplicably don't want a tonne of compost on their lawn.

Seeing such an impressive steaming pile of rotting plants, Theresa the Turkey cannot help but swoon.

Inside the compost, an exothermic reaction is well underway. Bonds between molecules are made, releasing heat. It is the perfect place for Terence and Theresa to raise their eggs.

With the compost doing the incubation, both turkeys are free to enjoy each other's company, stroll the bush in romantic contemplation and terrorize any human interlopers.

ENDOTHERMIC REACTIONS

What if the opposite happened?

What if, instead of switching to new bonds that need less energy, the reaction makes bonds that release less energy?

This is what is called an **endothermic reaction**, and it sucks in energy.

In your daily life, endothermic reactions are rare. So rare that they feel strange – weird, even.

Imagine if a fireplace made the room colder, or if you went for a run and had to put on a jumper midway through the toughest bit?

Or even, if instead of gently warming the brush-turkey eggs, the compost heap chilled them?

Of course, we have devices that make us cooler, such as air conditioners or freezers, but they don't rely on chemical reactions.

Just occasionally, though, we do make use of cooling reactions. If you put ammonium nitrate into water, it goes cold very fast: the reaction sucks in heat.

This does have a few applications. It is used in cool packs, for soothing footballing injuries on the touch line. And also in cool packs you can buy to wrap around bottles and chill drinks on a picnic.

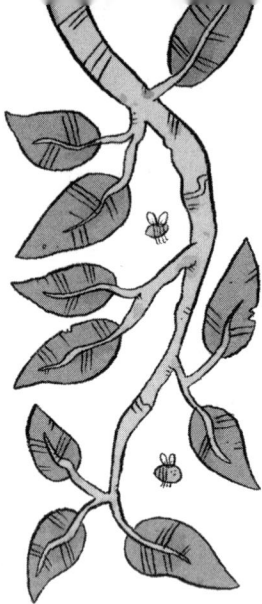

IS THAT IT FOR ENDOTHERMIC REACTIONS?

There is also one other reaction, arguably even more important than one that makes your drinks cool.

It involves a molecule that is very good at taking energy from sunlight, and using it to convert carbon dioxide into sugar and oxygen: **photosynthesis**.

Before that compost was releasing energy, it was absorbing it, in an endothermic reaction.

And without that particular endothermic reaction there would be no plants, no brush-turkeys – and no people to get annoyed when they build a nest on their lovely lawn.

RATES OF REACTION

In 2016, something astonishing happened in a Japanese plastic-recycling plant.

Among the discarded bottles, slowly discolouring in the sun, a new kind of bacteria was found: a bacteria that could eat plastic.

Evolution is about taking advantage of changing circumstances to find energy, reproduce and thrive. Which is exactly what this bacteria had done.

The reason plastic takes decades and centuries to be broken down by natural processes, polluting the environment in the process, is not because there is anything especially resilient about it.

It is because it is completely artificial – and, until 100 years ago, nature had never seen anything like it. Nothing had adapted to use it.

But that does not mean using it is impossible: there was a time in the history of the planet when nothing had adapted to use oxygen, either.

FINDING YOUR NICHE

As one scientist put it when the bacteria was discovered, "If you are a bacteria in a recycling plant and suddenly you are able to eat something no one else can, it's a huge advantage."

Not just for the bacteria: breaking down plastics is also one of the great goals of environmentalists.

So how could we do the same?

When researchers began investigating how the bacteria did it, they found they had evolved an enzyme – which is a biological version of something called a **catalyst**.

Catalysts are unusual, in that they help reactions but aren't used up in them. Instead, they speed them up: sometimes dramatically.

To make bread from wheat, humans use catalysts in yeast to break down the sugars in flour.

To make the ammonia used in fertilizer, we use an iron catalyst to join together nitrogen and hydrogen.

In both cases, the reaction goes a lot faster ... but the catalyst is unaffected.

Quite how dramatically these can change reactions is shown by what the Japanese bacteria achieved with their catalyst.

They were able to take a process that normally takes decades or more, and made it happen in days.

TO GO FASTER, HEAT IT

Catalysts are useful, but they are not the only way to speed up a reaction.

Reactions happen, in the most fundamental sense, because the reacting chemicals bump into each other.

If you want the reaction to be speedier, a good start is to make that bumping happen more often – you aren't going to, say, make carbon dioxide without a carbon atom hitting an oxygen atom.

What's a good way to make atoms collide?

Make them move faster.

And how do you do that?

In Chemistry, the average speed of the atoms in a substance has a different name: temperature. And heat is just a measure of the jiggliness of atoms.

So to make them speedier, heat them.

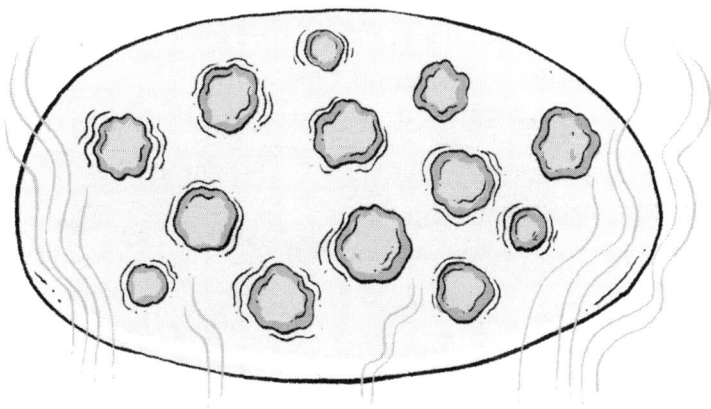

TO GO EVEN FASTER, CHOP IT

You can heat something as hot as you like, and its atoms can jiggle faster and faster. But if most of those atoms never hit the substance they are meant to be reacting with, it's all for nothing.

To make sure that can happen, you can increase the surface area of the reactants.

If you sink an iron ship, a century later you still have a hunk of rusting metal.

If you scatter iron filings in the sea, a century later you have nothing.

If you try to set fire to bread, you get toast.

If you try to set fire to a cloud of the flour that makes the bread (don't do this), you get an explosion.

So, if scientists ever do harness the plastic-catalyst, they will also do two other things before using it: grind up the bottles to increase the surface area, and warm everything up.

TO SPEED UP A REACTION:

- Chop it up.
- Heat it up.

Add a catalyst.

REVERSIBLE REACTIONS

You can't unboil an egg. Reactions go one way – but not the other.

Or do they?

In 1798 Claude Louis Berthollet, one of the French Emperor Napoleon's chemists, was sitting by a lake in Egypt.

At the time, everyone thought reactions only happened in one direction. You can, for instance, burn a log of wood to make smoke, but you could never collect smoke and make a log of wood.

But Berthollet noticed something unusual at the edge of the lake: a crust of sodium carbonate.

This wasn't what should have happened. It was, in fact, the equivalent of making a log from smoke.

The lake was a soda lake, which meant it was very salty. This was because it drew minerals from the surrounding rocks and then the water kept evaporating in the heat – ratcheting up their concentration.

Berthollet knew this lake contained sodium carbonate and calcium chloride.

He also knew that these reacted to form sodium chloride and calcium carbonate.

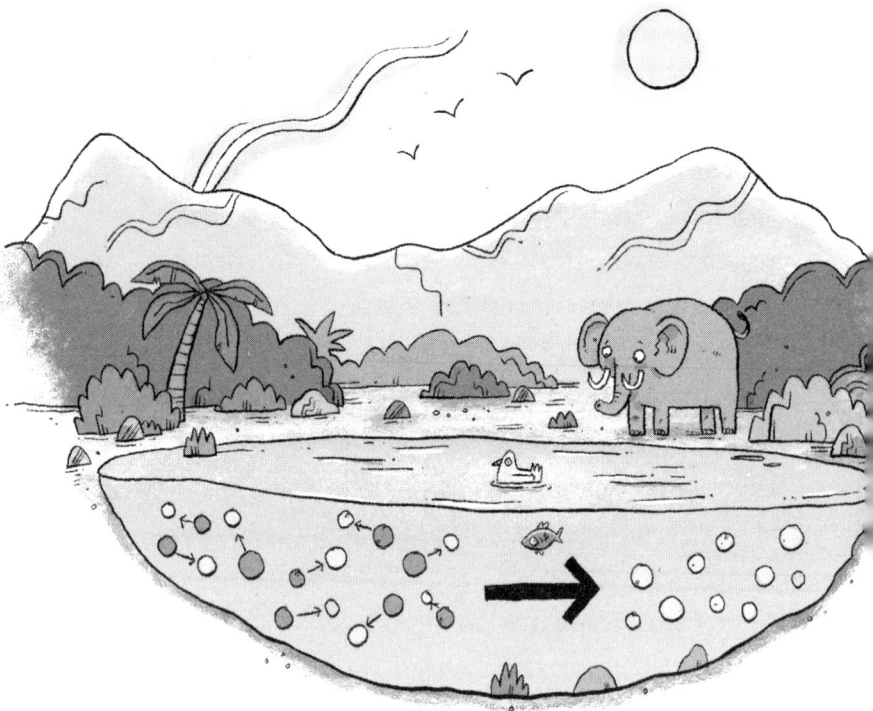

**Sodium carbonate and calcium carbonate making
sodium chloride and calcium carbonate**

There shouldn't have been any sodium carbonate left, yet here it was.

Then Berthollet realized something: the lake was not just very salty, but, as it evaporated in the desert heat, it was getting saltier.

We think of reactions as only going one way.

Iron and oxygen come together to make iron oxide, or rust.

Carbon in wood and oxygen in the air come together to make carbon dioxide.

What if that wasn't the whole story?

What if, normally, a reaction went one way, but in some cases, if it got too concentrated, it then went the other?

It sounds silly – a bit like saying that, if there were too much carbon dioxide in the air, then burning wood would make it gain carbon rather than losing it.

But, in this lake, that was what was happening.

Later, chemists would work out formally what was happening.

Some reactions go in both directions all the time. In the lake, at the same time as sodium carbonate and calcium chloride were reacting to make sodium chloride and calcium carbonate, the opposite was happening too.

When there wasn't much of the sodium chloride and calcium carbonate, you don't notice this – the first reaction overwhelms everything.

But as the concentration of those two chemicals increases, then the second reaction, going in the

opposite direction to the first, becomes
more noticeable.

Eventually, it happens at the same rate.

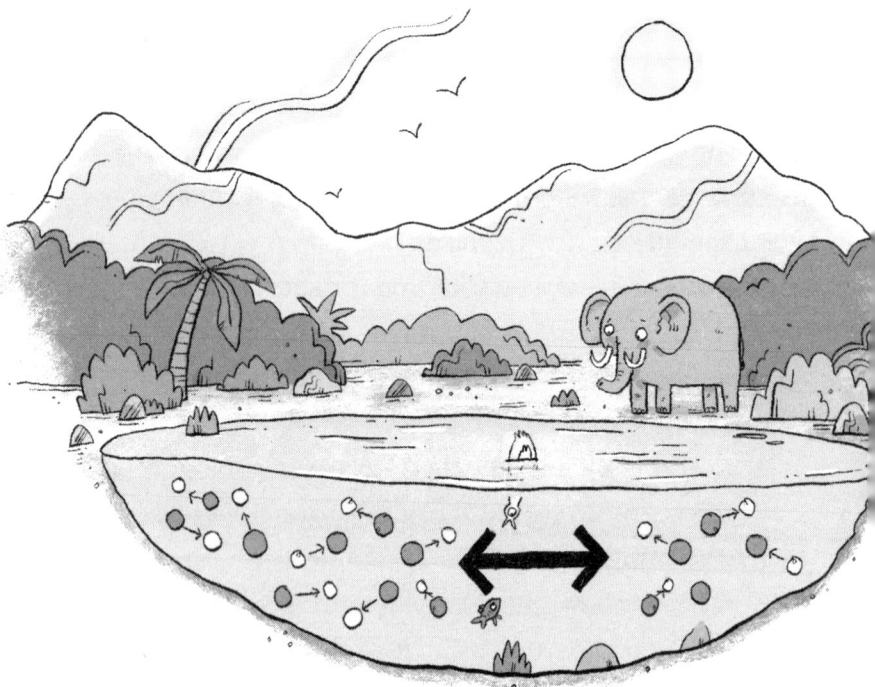

**Sodium carbonate and calcium chloride making sodium chloride
and calcium carbonate *and* sodium chloride and calcium carbonate
making sodium carbonate and calcium chloride**

Above that concentration, which is known as the
equilibrium position, the reaction predominantly
goes in the other direction – it appears to go
in reverse, like carbon coming out of the sky to
make wood.

But that is not the only thing that is opposite. If, in one direction, the reaction is **exothermic**, in the other, it is **endothermic**.

By the way, in 2015, scientists *did* succeed in unboiling an egg.

Their very complicated experiment managed to untangle the proteins of a boiled egg, to produce the mixture they started with.

Although, for any experimental chefs starting to get over-excited, you should know there's a catch.

The unboiling process involved mixing the cooked eggs with urea – one of the components of wee. Yum.

IN SHORT: Don't react badly; reactions aren't that complicated.

WHAT YOU NEED TO KNOW

- Exothermic reactions give out heat, meaning that the bonds made in the reaction give out more energy than the bonds broken take in.
- Endothermic reactions take in heat, meaning that the bonds made in the reaction give out less energy than the bonds broken take in.
- Reactions, whether exothermic or endothermic, often need activation energy – such as initially heating them up – to get started.
- Some reactions are reversible. Normally they may go from chemical A to chemical B, but when a certain proportion of chemical B is reached, they do the reverse.
- Reactions go faster with catalysts, when there is more surface area of the chemicals being reacted, and with heating.

TIME-TRAVELLING CHEMISTRY, PART 5: FERTILIZER

Clare's new Stone Age acquaintances are what, 300,000 years in the future, anthropologists will refer to as a "hunter-gatherer society".

The clue is in the name: they hunt, they gather. Each morning, they set off for work – trekking through the forest, stalking prey or grubbing through the bushes to find fruit and nuts.

After several weeks of living off her pottery-and-fire glory, to her slight annoyance, Clare has picked up on a growing implication that she should – well – help out a bit.

There have been knowing glances when the meat is passed round, and meaningful sighs when a gathering party returns to find her cooling her feet in a pot, while trying to persuade one of the children to fan her.

But, Clare thought to herself, she was not a girl who trekked. She had seen the state of the others' feet and, frankly, callouses were not for her.

Chomping idly on a banana, ignoring the glowering of the woman who picked it, she realizes there is a solution – agriculture.

Why search for food, when you can grow it at the cave mouth?

That's when Clare begins her garden, collecting pips and planting them around the cave.

She watches with joy as they sprout, green shoots of hope reaching for the sun. Carefully she tends them, as the delicate fronds sway in the breeze.

Then she watches as, one-by-one, they die.

They need something more. They need nutrients. They need, Clare decides, wee.

After water, sunlight and carbon dioxide, one of the most important chemicals you can give plants is nitrogen.

Nitrogen is what they use to make chlorophyll, the substance that converts sunlight to energy. Without nitrogen, they die; with it, they thrive.

The good news is, nitrogen is everywhere – there is far more of it in the air than any other gas.

The bad news is, it is difficult for plants to get it from the atmosphere.

It is very easy for them to harvest it from the soil though.

And an easy way to make a form that goes into the soil? Excrete it.

In wee, there is a substance called urea. Urea is something bodies don't need, which is why they get rid of it in urine.

But it is something plants very much need – the formula of urea is CH_4N_2O, and it contains a lot of nitrogen.

Generally, depending on how salty the wee is, it is recommended to dilute it with six parts water – roughly the ratio you use when making orange squash.

Then splash liberally over the soil, and watch plants bulk out.

After several days of making the Stone Agers drink water continuously, then relieve themselves in her garden – not something that especially improved relations – Clare has an even better idea.

Wee is not her only source of nitrogen, because humans are not the only animals that excrete nitrogen: so do birds and bats.

In the nineteenth century, before the invention of the Haber process (see Chapter Nine), this made bird poo one of the most important resources on the planet.

On rocky islands in the Pacific, where generations of birds had pooed for millennia, entire mining operations were set up to export it.

And at the back of Clare's cave, where bats have also been pooing for millennia, she has the same resource.

(And it can be exploited without awkwardly miming actions she really would rather not mime.)

Over the months that follow – months of shovelling bat poo and weeing into pots – the tender shoots become hardy plants and, finally, fruit-laden bushes.

No more do the Stone Agers have to search the jungle for food: the food comes to them. And, just as importantly, thinks Clare, it comes to her.

But these days, given the secret ingredient, she just makes double-sure to wash it first.

CHAPTER 6

ELECTRO-CHEMISTRY

INTRODUCTION
ELECTRO-CHEMISTRY

IN THIS CHAPTER YOU WILL LEARN ABOUT:

- Batteries
- Electrolysis
- Fuel cells
- Oxidation and reduction

BEFORE YOU READ THIS CHAPTER:

It is, perhaps, the most famous scene in science fiction. Victor Frankenstein stands over a lifeless corpse, stitched together from grave-robbed body parts; then he flicks a switch and puts the "spark of being" into its cadaverous flesh ... and his monster twitches.

With that flow of electricity – a mysterious energy, at the time – he had created life. He had changed inanimate matter into something that could move and think.

These days, we don't often think of electricity as being much of a force for change, unless it is changing bread into toast in our toaster.

We also know it is not a "vital force", as some thought in the nineteenth century. Instead, it is the flow of electrons: the movement of particles.

And not long after Mary Shelley, the *Frankenstein* author, was imagining ways electricity could make monsters, scientists showed it could make something far more useful: chemical apparatus that change one particle into another.

It can take ions out of solution and make them appear as pure solids – or as pure gases bubbling up – in an experiment worthy of Frankenstein.

If electricity can be used to change particles, the reverse is also true: changing and moving particles can be used to make electricity.

We do this in an electrical device we call a battery.

This chapter is about the place where Chemistry meets Physics; where Frankenstein's "spark of being" becomes involved in chemical reactions.

BATTERIES

The jar was dusty and chipped. The metal rod was rusted and lumpy. Beside it was a dull metal tube, tarnished and dented.

Amid all the splendours of ancient Mesopotamia – the culture where human civilization began, where scribes created the first writing and astronomers first catalogued the heavens – it was difficult to see what set these artefacts apart.

But when Wilhelm König, a German archaeologist, happened upon them in 1938, he thought differently.

He thought that, in these simple 2,000 year-old objects, there was more ingenuity than in the famed ziggurat temples of nearby Ur; and more evidence of human creativity than in the exquisite Mesopotamian artworks those temples contained.

The reason why – a reason he spotted where many, if not most, archaeologists would not – comes in how they join together.

The tube fits snugly in the mouth of the jar. The iron rod fits inside that, without, crucially, touching the sides. And, König saw when he looked more closely, it was corroded as if it had been in contact with an acid.

It was, he declared, a **battery**.

Batteries, today, are phenomenally complex.

The Chemistry and Physics involved in making the kind of light and powerful device that provides the energy for a phone has cost billions of pounds to develop.

But they are still also, fundamentally, just three things: two different metals, called **electrodes**, and an **electrolyte**, which is a liquid containing charged particles or ions.

Getting these things together is surprisingly easy to achieve.

A lemon, for instance, contains an acid: an electrolyte. Stick a bit of copper in one side of it and a bit of iron in the other, join them with a wire, and electricity flows. You have a battery.

Potatoes, oranges, and even cactuses produce the same effect.

How does it do it? It is not magic, although it seems like it – and certainly would have done so 2,000 years ago.

Scientists are obsessed with energy. One of the absolute rules of Physics and Chemistry is that energy cannot be created or destroyed. The same is true in a battery.

Energy is not being produced from nowhere. Instead, what is really happening is that the more reactive metal – the copper – is, in a sense, reacting with the other one – the iron.

It was not until the modern age that humans began to exploit this. At least, that was what people thought, until König found the artefact which is now known as the Baghdad Battery.

His idea was this. With the metals in place, the jar would be filled with an acid such as vinegar. Then, the iron would act as one electrode and the copper as another.

Between the two, a wire would pass – and electricity would flow.

The voltage you get depends on the difference in reactivity of the metals used.

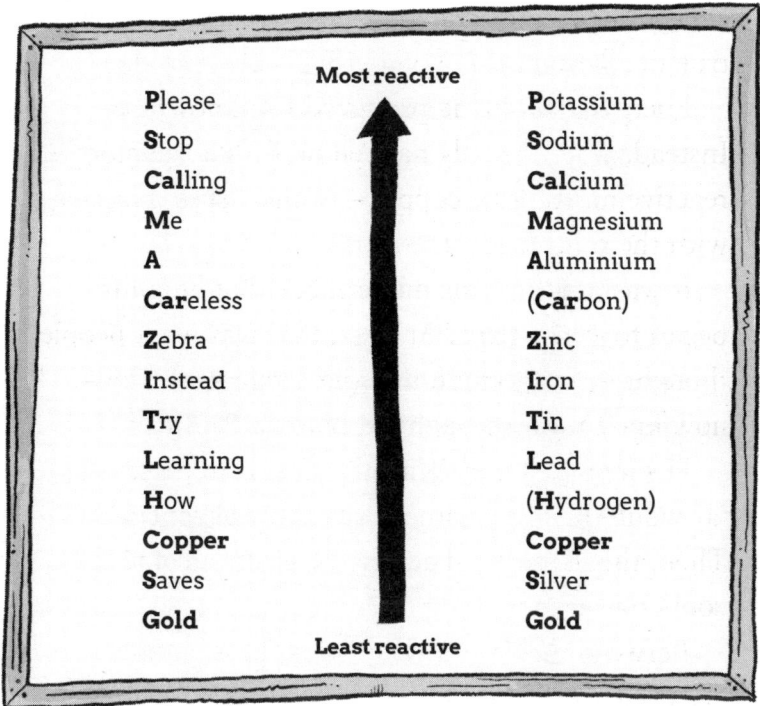

	Most reactive ↑	
Please		**P**otassium
Stop		**S**odium
Calling		**Ca**lcium
Me		**M**agnesium
A		**A**luminium
Careless		(**Car**bon)
Zebra		**Z**inc
Instead		**I**ron
Tin		**Ti**n
Learning		**L**ead
How		(**H**ydrogen)
Copper		**Copper**
Saves		**S**ilver
Gold	↓ Least reactive	**Gold**

Not everyone agrees with his interpretation. True, modern versions of the Baghdad battery have been built, and then used to make electricity. So it could have worked that way.

The question is though, did it?

Just because it is possible to use the artefact to make electricity does not mean that that was what it actually did.

Not least because, what would be the point? If Baghdad had no electrical appliances, what use had it for electricity?

This question is unanswerable – but that does not stop archaeologists suggesting some possible applications.

The first is medicinal. The Greeks liked to apply electric fish to their feet to cure pain. Maybe this was a more portable solution, for a desert culture with an electric fish shortage?

Another suggestion, though, is straightforward trickery. That is the one favoured by Paul Craddock, an expert based at the British Museum.

"I have always suspected you would get tricks done in the temple," he said. "The statue of a god could be wired up, and then the priest would ask you questions.

"If you gave the wrong answer, you'd touch the statue and would get a minor shock – along with, perhaps, a small mysterious blue flash of light.

"Get the answer right, and the trickster or priest could disconnect the batteries and no shock would arrive.

"The person would then be convinced of the power of the statue, priest and the religion."

FUEL CELL

Batteries are not the only way to make electricity. Fuel cells do too. And, along the way, they also make water. They work by uniting hydrogen and oxygen and then, sneakily, intercepting some of the electrons involved in the reaction.

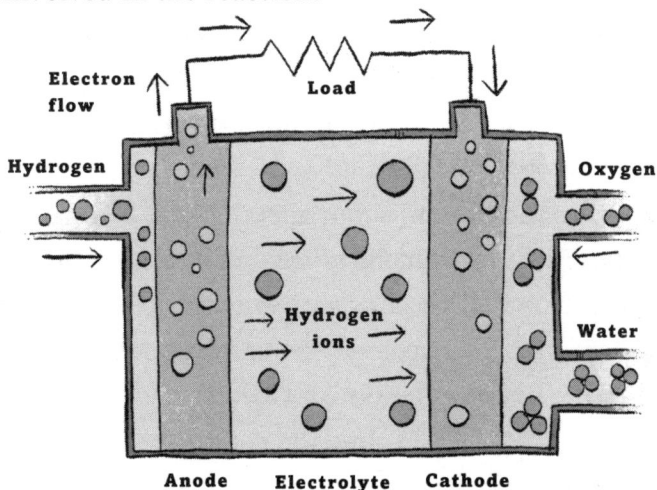

1. In the first part of the fuel cell, hydrogen is made to lose its electrons – producing hydrogen ions (and, you'll remember from Chapter Four, an acid).
2. Those hydrogen ions and electrons whizz to the other side of the cell, where they join with oxygen. But, they don't take the same path.
3. The ions can pass through the liquid but the only route the electrons can take is along a wire – where they are used as electricity.

ELECTROLYSIS

In June, 1808, the hottest ticket in London was at the Royal Institution. There, a scientific superstar was set to give a talk on his latest findings.

Sir Humphry Davy did not disappoint. Standing in front of an audience of excited aristocrats, dressed in their finery, his assistant wheeled in a vast battery.

Then, Davy placed its two wires in a silvery liquid – and the crowd watched in awe as a kind of chemical magic occurred.

At one of the wires, a new metal accumulated. At the other there was a continuous bubbling.

The reason Davy's lectures were so popular was not just because he was one of the finest chemists in history. In fact, that probably had very little to do with it.

It was because he was a lot of fun.

When he was little, he and his sister Kitty worked together making explosives and conducting all sorts of experiments. He used to scare his other siblings by drawing phosphorescent figures on their walls, that would glow ghoulishly in the dark.

His great contribution to Chemistry was to isolate nine elements, including potassium and chlorine.

But he spent a large part of his career distracted by nitrous oxide – better known (because of him) as laughing gas.

He was reputedly the first to inhale this gas, which gets you temporarily drunk, and he had so much fun when he did that he kept going.

Soon, there was a fashion for laughing gas parties among the British upper class.

This was a time when science was seen as both an exciting cultural activity – and one that it was necessary to understand, if you were to call yourself an intellectual.

Coleridge, the poet, began his studies of the subject with the statement, "I shall attack Chemistry, like a Shark!"

That June day in 1808, the audience were having a great time, but it was not because of laughing gas – it was because they, like Coleridge, were learning serious, cutting-edge science.

The technical explanation of what was going on was that Davy was using electrolysis to separate out an ionic compound.

One of those present had another interpretation: it was nigh-on sorcery.

"There stood Davy," wrote audience member Thomas Dibdin, "as the mighty magician of nature… The hardest metals melted like wax beneath its operation.

"The tremendous force of such an agency struck the learned with delight, and the unlearned with mingled rapture and astonishment; and the theatre or lecture-room rung with applause."

Electrolysis works a little like a battery, but in reverse.

In the electrolyte, there are two types of ion: one positive and one negative. (In Davy's case, the ions were of oxygen and a metal such as magnesium.)

The positive ions are looking for an excuse to gain electrons, something known as reduction. The negative ones are looking for an excuse to lose them – which is called oxidation (although, confusingly, it doesn't always involve oxygen).

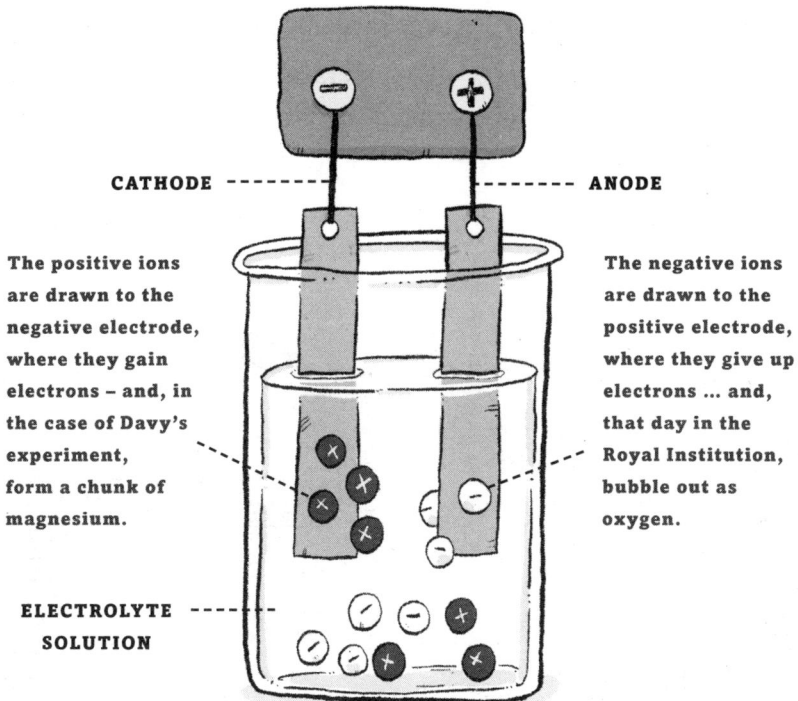

CATHODE -------- -------- ANODE

The positive ions are drawn to the negative electrode, where they gain electrons – and, in the case of Davy's experiment, form a chunk of magnesium.

The negative ions are drawn to the positive electrode, where they give up electrons ... and, that day in the Royal Institution, bubble out as oxygen.

ELECTROLYTE SOLUTION

SPACE CHEMISTRY

On the International Space Station, everything is recycled – including water.

Sweat, urine and waste water are all cleaned and turned into something drinkable. Or, in the words of one astronaut, "yesterday's coffee is today's coffee".

That's not actually always true though. Because, after the water is recycled, some is converted into something even more precious: oxygen. And this is done through electrolysis.

Water exists as the molecule H_2O but, slightly confusingly, it also forms a solution with itself; within a glass of water there are also H+ and OH- ions.

A small quantity of the atoms form ions, with the result being that water can conduct electricity.

This means that, just like anything else with ions, if you put a cathode and an anode in it, it will separate these ions out.

In this way, the International Space Station can use electricity from its solar panels to turn water into hydrogen and oxygen.

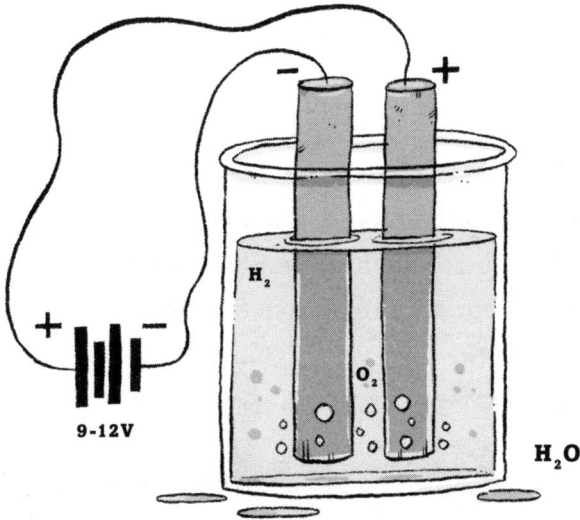

The oxygen is used for breathing, while the hydrogen is recombined with carbon dioxide breathed out by the astronauts ... to make water, which is again used to make coffee, which is used to make wee, which is used to make coffee.

Such is the glamour of space travel.

IN SHORT: Is Chemistry boring? No! It's electrifying.

WHAT YOU NEED TO KNOW:

- Batteries, also known as chemical cells, need three things: two electrodes, made from different metals, and a liquid with ions in – known as an electrolyte. A chemical reaction means that electrons gather at one of the electrodes, so one is positive and one negative.
- Fuel cells take in hydrogen and oxygen to make water, and a voltage.
- In electrolysis, there are also electrodes, connected by an ionic liquid or solution. The electrodes donate or receive electrons from the ions in the liquid, which then form as pure elements.
- Oxidation involves losing electrons, reduction involves gaining them.

TIME-TRAVELLING CHEMISTRY, PART 6: WATER PURIFICATION

The downside of being viewed as a technological magician from the future, Clare finds, is that people blame her for things.

There has been an outbreak of dodgy tummies in the cave, and with it has come a distinctly frosty air.

As the Stone Agers run to the pit outside, holding their stomachs, Clare gets the distinct impression they suspect her – and her new-fangled inventions – might be to blame.

She needs an improvement in sanitation, and fast. It is time to start purifying the water.

The best way to clean water is to boil it. But it takes effort to heat it, it takes time to cool it, and pottery has a tendency to break in the process.

So, she has a different idea. It still involves pottery, it still requires charcoal – but this time, she's not going to burn the charcoal. She's going to turn it into a filter.

There is a particular kind of charcoal known as activated charcoal, which sounds more dramatic than it actually is.

If you take normal charcoal and put it back in a kiln, but this time spray the bottom of the kiln with water, something almost magical happens.

In an atmosphere of steam, all the tiny particles of trapped organic material caught within the charcoal are burned off.

What is left behind are holes – thousands of them.

The network of holes inside this "activated" charcoal is so extensive that a single gram has a surface area similar to a football pitch.

And using this vast surface area, the charcoal is able to pick up contaminants. They get caught in its holes, they stick to its cavities – and all that is left afterwards is pure water.

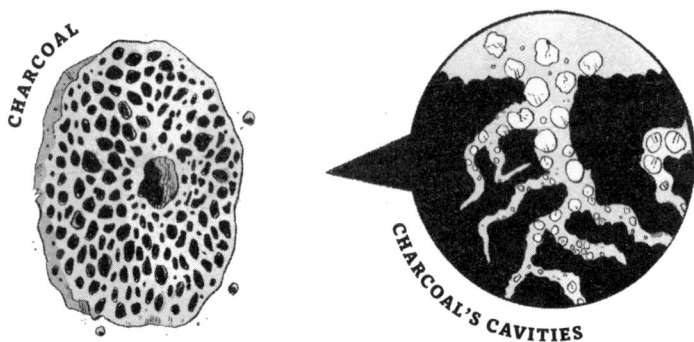

CHARCOAL

CHARCOAL'S CAVITIES

All Clare needs to then do is turn one of the pots into a rudimentary filter: put a hole at the base, add a good layer of crumbled charcoal at the top, pour in water … and she finds that what comes out of the bottom is clean.

Another problem solved!

CHAPTER 7

ORGANIC CHEMISTRY

INTRODUCTION
ORGANIC CHEMISTRY

IN THIS CHAPTER YOU WILL LEARN ABOUT:

- Hydrocarbons
- Alcohols
- Carboxylic acids
- Polymers and polyesters

BEFORE YOU READ THIS CHAPTER:

When astronomers look towards distant planets, seeking out signs of alien life, they do not make many assumptions about the creatures looking back at them.

They might be friendly, they might be murderous. They might have two arms, eight arms or no arms. They might live in the sea, roam the land or float in the air.

Most likely, they will be like nothing we have seen, let alone imagined.

There is, however, one bet that most astronomers will make: alien life, like all life on Earth, will be carbon-based.

Carbon is light, it is abundant, and – most important of all when it comes to life – it bonds with lots of other elements in lots of different ways. So far, ten million different carbon compounds have been found.

It is from this vast chemical toolkit that life is created; to make the enzymes, proteins and sugars that keep it going. From Venus fly-traps to velociraptors, everything that lives now, and that has ever lived, on Planet Earth does so by manipulating this one element.

This is why, although carbon is just one of more than 100 elements, it deserves a branch of Chemistry all of its own: **Organic Chemistry**.

A FIRE TEMPLE ... AND HYDROCARBONS

At the easternmost tip of Azerbaijan, where the land juts into the Caspian Sea, fire comes out of the ground. Here, for at least a millennium, people have come to worship the sacred eternal flames.

To reach the fire temple, built on the site in the seventeenth century, pilgrims have to walk over other unusual – but far less interesting – natural wonders.

And they will almost certainly pay less mind to the black, oozing liquid coming from the ground, all along their route, than the dazzling prospect of the mysterious flames.

But the secret behind the flames lies in that liquid: it is crude oil. So rich is the Caspian Sea in oil, that it just seeps from the soil.

And so, too, does natural gas.

Superficially, the two seem very different. One is a glutinous treacle that bubbles up from the ground; the other is an invisible gas that jets into the atmosphere and that once lit – whether on a cooker or a sacred peninsula – stays lit.

But really, they are different arrangements of the same atoms. And they are both **hydrocarbons**: molecules of hydrogen and carbon.

There are lots of different kinds of hydrocarbon. Some, such as **octane**, are liquid and used in petrol engines. Others, such as **butane**, are gases at room temperature and used in camping fuel.

They are not only useful for burning though. Hydrocarbons are the basis of plastics, detergents, lubricants, cosmetics and many other everyday products.

Most types will be contained in that crude oil, bubbling up beneath the pilgrims' feet.

To make it useful, you have to split the crude oil into each type, so that they can be used individually in their purest form.

ALKANES

A lot of crude oil comes in the form of **alkanes**. These are molecules with twice as many hydrogen atoms as carbon, and then two more.

So, for instance, the simplest alkane is methane – CH_4

The next simplest is **ethane**. It has two carbons, so must have 6 hydrogens (as **2 x 2 + 2 is 6**).

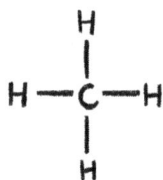 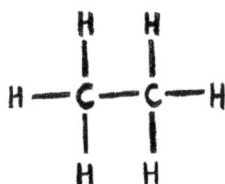 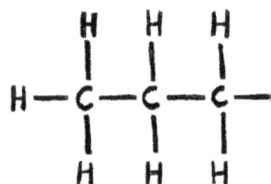

METHANE   ETHANE   PROPANE

In general, the alkanes have the formula: C_nH_{2n+2}.

The fewer carbon atoms they have, the smaller the molecules and the easier it is for them to break out of their liquid form and become a gas. Or, in Chemistry terms, the lower their boiling point.

This is why methane, which was what started the fires in Azerbaijan, is a gas when found in the natural world.

The bigger, heavier molecules stay liquid though – their boiling point is higher.

This property gives a clue as to how we can separate crude oil, which is a soup of hydrocarbons jumbled together, into its different parts.

We do this using a process called fractional distillation. If you scoop up some oil and heat it, different alkanes will boil off at different temperatures.

It is likely that in the summer in Azerbaijan, when temperatures top 40 degrees Celsius, this process starts to begin – with pentane, the lightest alkane that is liquid at room temperature, evaporating from the liquid.

Crucially, they will also condense back into liquids at different temperatures too. (This is the principle behind fractional distillation.)

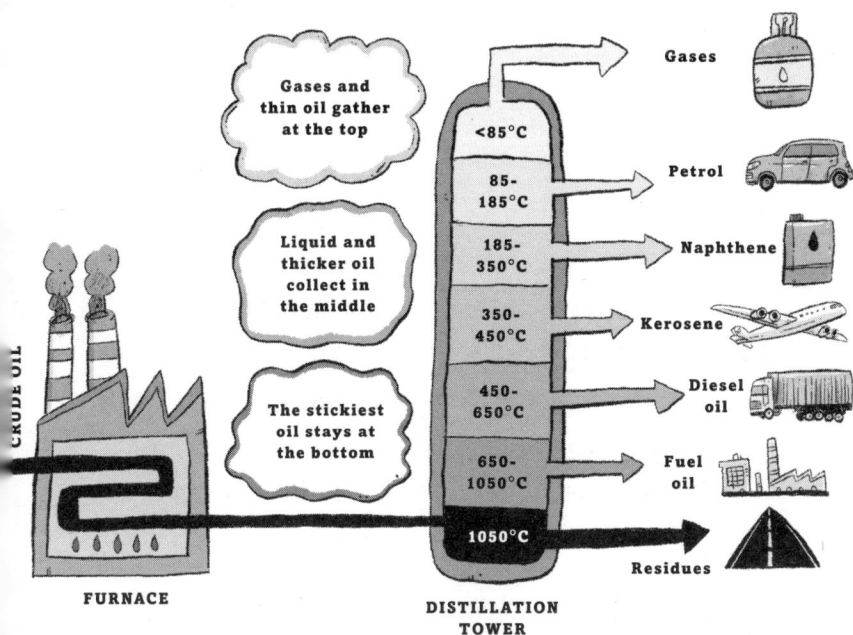

Gases and thin oil gather at the top

Liquid and thicker oil collect in the middle

The stickiest oil stays at the bottom

CRUDE OIL

FURNACE

DISTILLATION TOWER

<85°C — Gases

85-185°C — Petrol

185-350°C — Naphthene

350-450°C — Kerosene

450-650°C — Diesel oil

650-1050°C — Fuel oil

1050°C — Residues

These days, the sacred and eternal fires of Azerbaijan are a fair bit less eternal. In fact, in 1969 they stopped entirely.

In Baku, the country's capital, too much gas had been pumped out of the ground to be used in industry, and there wasn't enough to keep the fire temple running.

Today, the flames are back – but only because the gas is taken off the grid that supplies homes and businesses, and piped in for the benefit of tourists and worshippers.

CRACKING

The longer the chain of hydrocarbons, the less useful it is. Longer hydrocarbons – which are those with more atoms in them – have a higher boiling point and are less unstable, making them less effective as fuels.

Cracking is a way of turning long hydrocarbons into short ones. It involves heating the alkanes to 550 degrees Celsius and, normally, passing them over a catalyst (which you'll remember from Chapter Five).

The result is that those long chains of atoms split apart into smaller ones. At its simplest, a long alkane becomes a shorter alkane and also something else; something with a very slightly different name and a very slightly different formula too: an **alkene**.

Alkenes are like alkanes, but instead of having the formula C_nH_{2n+2}, they have the formula C_nH_{2n} – so, they have twice as many hydrogen as carbon.

For instance, **decane** ($C_{10}H_{22}$) might convert to octane (C_8H_{18}) and ethene (C_2H_4).

Decane $C_{10}H_{22}$

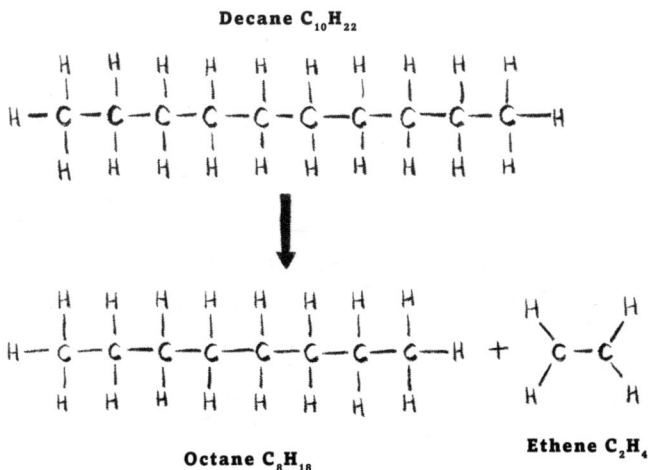

Octane C_8H_{18}

Ethene C_2H_4

You can also go the other way. Under some circumstances, an alkene will react with hydrogen to make an alkane. This is called hydrogenation.

It is useful to chemists, but it is also useful for food scientists. Hydrogenated fats, also known as saturated fats, last better than unhydrogenated (or unsaturated) ones, so foods containing them can be kept for longer on supermarket shelves.

The downside? They are probably worse for you, too.

ALCOHOLS

Between 1927 and 1933, the difference of two hydrogens and one carbon killed an estimated 10,000 people.

At the time, the US was engaging in one of the most ill-fated experiments in human history: Prohibition. Alcohol was banned across the country.

Or, at least, it was banned for drinking. The problem was, alcohol is extremely useful – so it was still needed by several different industries.

This led to a profitable business for chemists. They would take this industrial alcohol, convert it into something that was almost-but-not-quite a drinkable drink, and sell it on.

The government, still determined to keep a decidedly un-sober country sober, fought back. It added a poison called methanol to the pure alcohol used in industry, so that no one would drink it.

But they did anyway.

The poison added wasn't a traditional poison, like cyanide. It was, itself, alcohol.

All alcohols are poison, but not all alcohol is the same. Some alcohol is the kind of poison that will eventually kill you, but only after you have got quite

163

talkative, started singing, danced on a table, then passed out.

That is the kind of alcohol we call ethanol.

Ethanol – the active ingredient of gin and tonic, beer and wine – has been made by every civilization that has ever existed.

The reason behind this is that you can produce ethanol by chance. When something sugary, such as fruit, barley or even potato, is left around in the warmth, often microorganisms such as yeast will begin to digest it.

They will break down the sugar into carbon dioxide and ethanol; a substance with the formula C_2H_5OH.

Ethanol has lots of uses: in medicine, it is an antiseptic; in cosmetics it is used for a range of tasks, from helping clean skin to helping hair spray stick to hair. It can also be used as fuel, in paints and as de-icer for your car windscreen.

Yet, of all this, one use has remained by far its most popular: helping people dance worse.

NOT ALL ALCOHOLS ARE EQUAL

Just as there are lots of different types of alkane and alkene, there are also lots of different types of alcohol.

What unites them is that they start with a hydrocarbon containing twice as many hydrogens as carbons, then add one more hydrogen. Then, joined to that, they all end in OH.

NAME	MOLECULAR FORMULA	FULL STRUCTRUAL FORMULA
Methanol	CH_3OH	$H-\overset{\displaystyle H}{\underset{\displaystyle H}{C}}-OH$
Ethanol	C_2H_5OH	$H-\overset{\displaystyle H}{\underset{\displaystyle H}{C}}-\overset{\displaystyle H}{\underset{\displaystyle H}{C}}-OH$
Propan-1-ol	C_3H_7OH	$H-\overset{\displaystyle H}{\underset{\displaystyle H}{C}}-\overset{\displaystyle H}{\underset{\displaystyle H}{C}}-\overset{\displaystyle H}{\underset{\displaystyle H}{C}}-OH$
Butan-1-ol	C_4H_9OH	$H-\overset{\displaystyle H}{\underset{\displaystyle H}{C}}-\overset{\displaystyle H}{\underset{\displaystyle H}{C}}-\overset{\displaystyle H}{\underset{\displaystyle H}{C}}-\overset{\displaystyle H}{\underset{\displaystyle H}{C}}-OH$

Antifreeze

Beer

Medicine

Fuel

One of these alcohols, methanol, was what the US government added to its legal ethanol. In doing so, they turned a mild poison into a terrible poison.

Ethanol is a poison that, when taken in moderation, temporarily deactivates the parts of your brain that control inhibitions.

Methanol is just ethanol with two fewer hydrogens and one fewer carbon – but it will kill you. Even if you are lucky and only take it in moderation you should still expect it to destroy your optic nerve.

There's a reason we have the phrase "blind drunk".

CARBOXYLIC ACIDS

The auctioneers Sotheby's are no strangers to rare wine.

In 2018, they sold the most expensive bottle ever: a £400,000 1945 Romanée-Conti from Burgundy.

If you buy bottles from Sotheby's, they are able to guarantee that the wine is the genuine product, in its original bottle – and that its seller is the legal owner.

What they cannot always guarantee though is the

most important thing: does it taste nice?

In the course of 75 years, wine can change. Sometimes it mellows, sometimes it improves and sometimes it is stored badly and reacts with oxygen.

When your £400,000 bottle of wine oxidizes, Sotheby's has very specific advice: "Use it for salad dressing."

That's because it will have become a particular carboxylic acid – better known as vinegar.

Like the hydrocarbons and alcohols, carboxylic acids form a group. They have a varying number of hydrogens and carbons, with a COOH on the end.

Sometimes, carboxylic acids are useful. They can be reacted with alcohols to form **esters** – which have strong, often pleasant, smells and can be used in flavouring.

Sometimes, however, they are poured on lettuce, as you slowly weep into the most expensive salad in history.

POLYMERS AND POLYESTERS

In 1953, the regulars at The Eagle pub in Cambridge were having a quiet lunch when, from across the road, two scientists blundered in.

"We have discovered," they announced, "the secret of life." The drinkers may have been sceptical, but the pair – James Watson and Francis Crick – really had.

In the laboratory opposite they had built a model of the structure of DNA; the chemical that encodes the instructions for building everything from the smallest bacteria to the blue whale.

This was not all their own work though – not even close. Watson and Crick had been helped by hundreds of advances that had come before. They had needed the insights of a brilliant biologist called Maurice Wilkins, and the deductions of a very clever chemist called Rosalind Franklin. They also needed the competitive urge of knowing they were not alone. For over a decade, the hunt had been on among scientists for the code of life.

Throughout this time, scientists may not have known exactly what stored our genetic information, but they had slowly reached a consensus on what the storage method would look like.

The first crucial deduction was based on a rather

obvious fact: whatever it was that stored all the information that made us human had to be small.

Otherwise, this information couldn't fit inside us, let alone in the bugs and bacteria that also needed to pass on information every time they reproduced.

This presents a problem though – very small things don't last. When you get tiny, the random bouncing and jittering of particles starts to break things up.

So the information had to be stored in something that could survive this buffeting – that could retain its structure for a lifetime.

What does that? A single molecule.

H_2O, after all, doesn't suddenly break apart or lose some hydrogen for no reason. The forces linking its atoms keep it together.

The second deduction was that this molecule had to be changeable – different depending on the creature it was in. It needed to tell a human being to grow hair and fingernails, a blue whale to grow to the size of a house, and a snail to grow a shell.

Just as computer code has 1s and 0s, and the English language has 26 letters, it needed a chemical "alphabet" that could be combined in any order.

It needed to be, in other words, a **polymer**.

Polymers are strange molecules. They are a bit like chemical Lego – where you join together blocks to build a tower as high as you want.

The simplest polymers all use the same building block. One example of this is **polyethene,** also known as polythene. The "**ethene**" means that ethene is the building block, or **monomer**; the "**poly**" bit means there is lots of them.

POLYETHENE

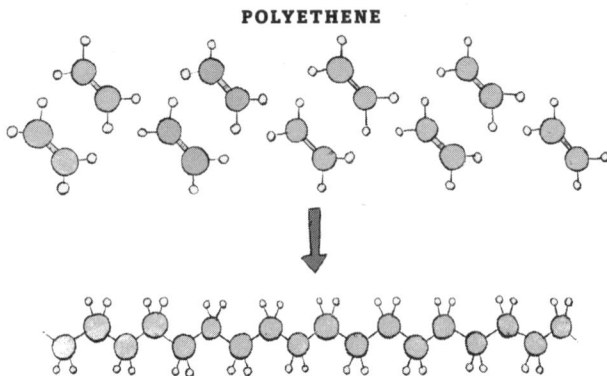

Instead of writing in all the atoms, which go on forever, this can be written just using its building block, ethene (which is called the monomer):

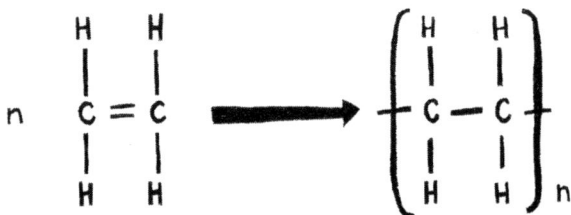

DNA

KEY:

Base pair

 **Thymine**

Cytosine

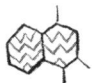 **Adenine**

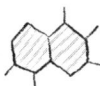 **Guanine**

Helix of sugar-phosphates

DNA is a lot more complicated than this. It uses four different building blocks, each of which will slot into the other.

Although, given that all polyethene has to make is a plastic bag, while DNA has to make the people who can imagine making plastic bags, four building blocks really isn't that much.

Particularly as, inside you, there is enough of it to stretch to the Sun – and back! – 60 times.

IN SHORT: A little bit of carbon goes a long way.

WHAT YOU NEED TO KNOW

- Oil is a mixture of different hydrocarbons – molecules made from hydrogen and carbon.
- The hydrocarbons come in different groups. Some, the alkenes, have twice as many hydrogen atoms as carbon atoms. So, butene is C_4H_8.
- The alkanes have two more hydrogens than the alkenes. So butane is C_4H_{10}.
- Oil is largely made up of alkanes.
- The more atoms in the molecule, the higher its boiling point.
- The different boiling points can be exploited to separate out hydrocarbons using fractional distillation.
- Bigger molecules can be broken down into alkanes and alkenes using a process called cracking.
- When hydrocarbons burn in oxygen they make carbon dioxide and water.
- Alcohols end in OH.
- Carboxylic acids are oxidized alcohols, and end in COOH.
- Polymers are really long molecules, made from repeated use of individual building blocks. They can be artificial or natural.

TIME-TRAVELLING CHEMISTRY, PART 7: BREAD

Days become weeks. Weeks become months. Clare settles in to the rhythm of a new life, a very different life – ruled by the sun and the rains, rather than the school bell.

Outside the cave, she takes satisfaction from her growing crops. Among them, she sees, are some grasses, their seeds blown in from the plains below. This gives her an idea.

You can speed up Chemistry, but you can't speed up Biology. Later, many generations later, these grasses will change.

Their descendants, chosen, selected and then bred over thousands of years of farming, will have evolved bigger and fatter seeds, held on stumpier bodies – and will be called wheat.

For now, though, the ancestors of wheat are more delicate and slender plants, with thin seeds designed to nourish a growing plant – not a growing human.

To collect enough to make bread would be a true labour of love, hours of boring effort that would certainly use up more calories than the food could replace.

But if there is one thing Clare now has, which she never used to have, it is time and patience.

Carefully, over the course of several days, she collects the ripened seeds. Between two large stones, she grinds them and removes the husks.

And what is left is a white powder: the world's first flour.

Flour might have never before been seen on the Earth, but the same is not true of the other key ingredient in making bread; the ingredient that adds the chemical magic. That ingredient has been around long before humans, and will be around long after.

Clare realizes that it is already there in her diet – right by the grasses, found in a thin, white fuzz that appears on the surface of some of the fruits.

It is yeast.

Making bread seems like a simple process, but Organic Chemistry is there from the beginning.

The first stage involves kneading together flour and water to make a dough. This is about so much more than just mixing: in the flour there are proteins called gluten. The water joins these together, bonding them with hydrogen.

And as Clare plunges her hand into the dough, squeezing and turning, the chains of gluten then uncoil – strengthening the mixture.

The water doesn't just bring the gluten together, it also mobilizes something called amylase. Inside the seeds is an energy source in the form of starch, which is used to give a head start to the plant's shoots.

Starch is essentially long chains of sugar molecules joined together. To break it apart – and get the sugary goodness – the plant uses amylase, a natural catalyst (see Chapter Five).

This is what also happens in the bread when you add water; the amylase gets to work, breaking down the starch. It is not the plant that will eat the sugar though, but the yeast that Clare has carefully scraped from the fruit.

Yeast is a fungus, and it feeds on sugar. Inside the dough, it begins to munch; in the process producing carbon dioxide and alcohol.

If you are using it to make beer, it's the alcohol you are interested in. In bread though, it's the carbon dioxide.

Trapped by the bubble-gum texture of the gluten, the gas has nowhere to go. Instead, it forms bubbles that slowly puff out the mixture as it is heated.

Clare watches as, inside her kiln, the dough begins to rise – and from out of it, there wafts a smell she thought she would never smell again: fresh bread.

PREHISTORIC BREAD RECIPE:

Ingredients

1. Lots of grass seeds.
2. More grass seeds.
3. Even more grass seeds.
4. You think you have enough grass seeds but you don't. Get more grass seeds.
5. Grass seeds really are very small compared to those in the wheat they will evolve into. Get more grass seeds.
6. Water.
7. Fungus (scrape it from some fruit).

Method

1. Grind the grass seeds between two stones until a white powder appears. This will be boring. Very boring.
2. Avoid any sabre-toothed tigers.
3. Mix with water, knead into dough.
4. Add fruit fungus, and bake in the oven.
5. Wait. You have no oven. First make oven.
6. Bake in oven.

CHAPTER 8

CHEMICAL ANALYSIS

INTRODUCTION
CHEMICAL ANALYSIS

IN THIS CHAPTER YOU WILL LEARN ABOUT:

- Chromatography
- Flame tests
- Spectroscopy
- Gas tests

Modern Chemistry allows us to calculate, with exquisite complexity, what it is that goes on when one substance reacts with another.

We know what happens when potassium is immersed in water; we know what happens (rather more slowly) when calcium carbonate is doused in acidic rain.

We know about electron shells and ionic bonds, about hydrocarbon cracking and exothermic reactions.

Yet all of this is useless, unless we also know one other, absolutely key thing: what the chemical we are using actually is.

If I give you, a chemist, a powdered-up substance, how do you work out what is in it?

To answer this question – which has embarrassed more than one chemist over the years – scientists have developed a whole series of tests, exploiting the different properties of different chemicals when you burn them, dissolve them and react them.

And they call this process **chemical analysis**.

THE CURIOUS CASE OF THE CHROMATOGRAPH AND THE SHOE

Sherlock Holmes had a keen eye for a muddy shoe. Famously, in the case of "The Five Orange Pips", he greeted a visitor with the words, "That clay and chalk mixture which I see upon your toe caps is quite distinctive."

(This is not the most charming way to say, "Hello, how are you?")

Later of course, as tended to be the case with apparently random details spotted in Sherlock Holmes mysteries, the particular mix of clay and chalk he saw would be crucial in solving the case.

As Watson explained, Holmes knew "at a glance different soils from each other. After walks, [he] has shown me splashes upon his trousers, and told me by their colour and consistence in what part of London he had received them."

It would take a century, but, today, even police without Holmes' astonishing deductive powers can solve crimes by studying soil.

They can do so thanks to a woman called Lorna Dawson, and a technique called chromatography.

Lorna Dawson was in her first year at Edinburgh University, when there was a particularly unpleasant murder nearby.

Two young women were seen leaving a pub with two men – and the next morning the women's bodies were found, dumped 8 km apart.

That was 1977, and the police were unable to solve the case. They had a suspect, but they could not tie him to the scene of the crime.

The years passed, and Dawson stayed in university and specialized in the analysis of soil. She gained respect in her field, and a professorship, but the murder of the women stayed with her.

"Fear gripped the community and spread right across Edinburgh, especially among young women," she recalled.

Over 30 years later, she was made to think about the case again, but this time as an expert witness.

Soil samples had been found on the foot of one of the victims. The court wanted to know if they could reveal where she had walked.

Dawson realized she could help – using chromatography.

Chromatography is a method for separating out the individual substances in a mixture. The simplest way uses paper.

Imagine you dissolve soil – or anything – in water or some other solvent. All of its individual components will have different solubility, meaning they require greater or lesser amounts of water to completely dissolve.

Now imagine you stick a dab of the soil on a strip of paper, then put the bottom of the paper in some water (or some other solvent), so it soaks it up. As the water rises, it will in theory deposit the molecules dissolved in it at different heights.

Where, precisely, it deposits them depends on how soluble the molecules are, and how attracted to the paper they are.

This means that each mixture leaves its own particular signature.

This signature describes what is in a solution.

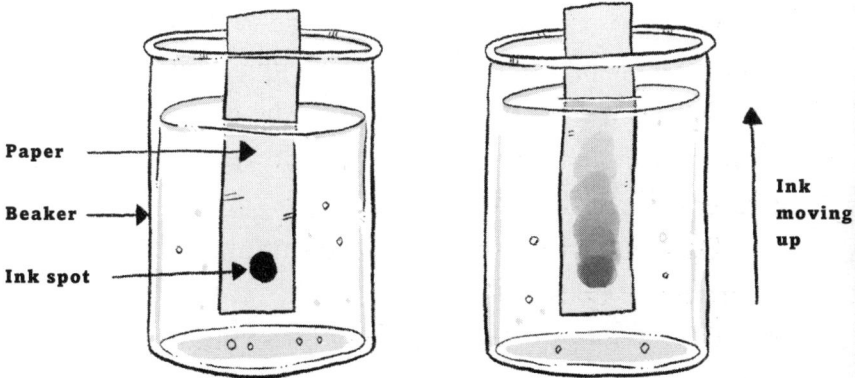

The paper is known as the "stationary phase", The water soaks into the paper and moves up it, so is called the "mobile phase".

In the case of soil, because the soil in each field is a unique mixture of different substances, this means a sample tells you where it is from.

In reality, this simplest method is hard to use for something as complex as soil – and is better on things like ink.

Although Professor Dawson used a more exacting version known as gas chromatography, the principles were the same.

When she analyzed the soil on the feet of one of the murdered women, she could construct their last steps – and show that the story told by the soil completely contradicted that told by the prime suspect.

After that it was, as Holmes might say, elementary.

FLAME TESTS

Queen Elizabeth I loved a good fireworks display.
So much so, in fact, that she created a new position
in her royal court.

Joining the chancellor and the privy councillors
in her employment was another great office of state:
fire master.

And the sole role of the fire master was to make
flamboyant fireworks to please the Queen.

Fireworks, by that time, were a Europe-wide
craze. Aristocrats competed to produce the best
displays, sometimes going a little too far.

Once, on a visit to Warwick, the local lord
was so keen to impress his Queen that he held a
mock battle in her honour, with cannons shooting
fireworks into sky.

Unfortunately, he was a bit overenthusiastic. As a chronicler recorded, "Whether by negligence or otherwise, it happened that a ball of fyre fell on a house."

Fireballs flew "over the Castell, and into the mydst of the towne ... to the great perill, or else great feare, of the inhabitants."

They were right to be afraid – at least one person was killed, and Elizabeth had to apologize and pay compensation.

But while that was undoubtedly a display that would have satisfied even the most pyrotechnically-minded queen (if not her cowering subjects), one thing was missing: colour.

All the fireworks, whether those impressing monarchs or those tumbling into houses, were white: made from exploding gunpowder.

It was not until the nineteenth century, that people witnessed the bursts of green, blue and red – popping up in the night sky like sudden-blooming flowers.

That was when the fire masters moved from being largely physicists (who understood rocketry) to being chemists too.

Compounds of different elements burn different colours.

Sodium compounds, for instance, burn with a yellow flame.

Strontium salts, on the other hand, are red.

Put these in a firework, and suddenly your bonfire night celebrations go from monochrome to technicolour.

But there are even more useful applications of this knowledge – at least, there are if you are a Chemistry student looking to work out the composition of mysterious substances.

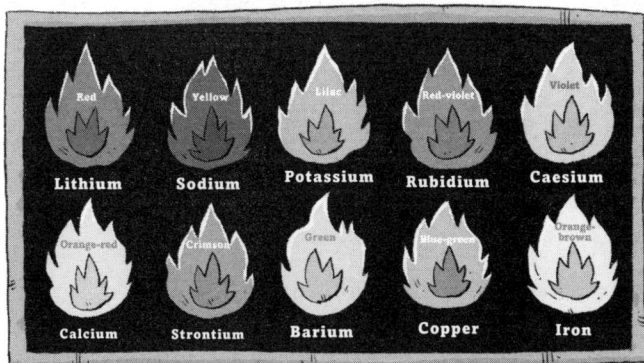

Red	Yellow	Lilac	Red-violet	Violet
Lithium	Sodium	Potassium	Rubidium	Caesium
Orange-red	Crimson	Green	Blue-green	Orange-brown
Calcium	Strontium	Barium	Copper	Iron

Metal ions produce different colours when they are heated in a flame. To test them, dip a wire loop in a sample of the compound, then place it in a Bunsen burner.

Flame tests are an easy way to tell compounds of metals apart.

They are also a way to produce fireworks displays that would have made even Queen Elizabeth I – a lady who had seen some pretty spectacular pyrotechnics – go "ooh".

TESTING FOR COMMON GASES

- Chlorine turns litmus paper white
- Oxygen relights a glowing splint
- Bubbling carbon dioxide through limewater turns the solution cloudy
- A test tube of hydrogen will make a squeak if you ignite it with a lit splint

SPECTROSCOPY

It had been a difficult few days for Pierre Janssen.

The Frenchman had travelled from France, taken a steamer across two oceans and round the Cape of Good Hope. He had landed in India and lugged crate-loads of scientific equipment inland.

Then, he had carefully aligned all the apparatus and set himself up at a temporary outpost in the town of Guntur – all to be in place for the 1868 solar eclipse.

But when he got there, the weather was stinking.

"It rained for many days… This rain was considered exceptional," he lamented.

Luckily, it lifted – almost miraculously – in time for the eclipse. At the very moment the Moon was set to align with the Sun, "He shone out in all his brilliancy."

Then Janssen watched as the Moon slowly ate a growing bite out of the Sun until all that was left was a bright circle enveloping a void.

That was when he saw something even more astonishing than an eclipse.

Janssen had travelled all that way because he knew that when all that was left of the Sun was a tiny sliver, he would be able to observe its atmosphere – unimpeded by the glare of the rest.

He had brought equipment that looked within that atmosphere for something called **spectral lines**.

When an atom is heated up – in a flame, or, say, the hottest object in the solar system – its electrons gain energy.

Or, to use the phrase of those scientists who study the subatomic world, they get "excited".

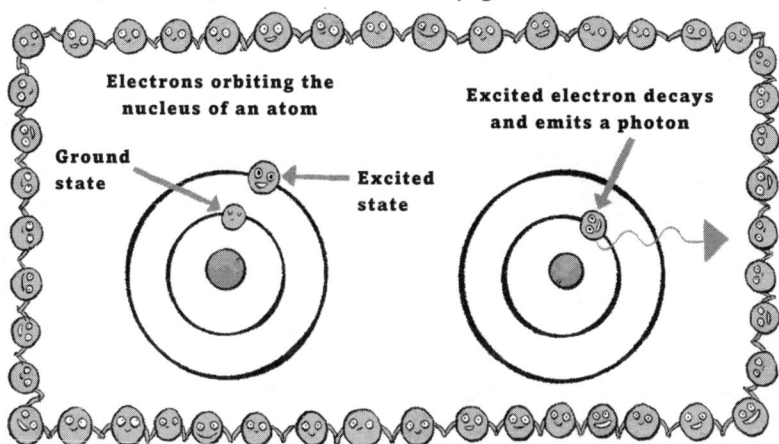

Electrons orbiting the nucleus of an atom

Excited electron decays and emits a photon

Ground state

Excited state

Excited electrons will occasionally drop down to a less excited level, but then emit that lost energy as light. The reverse is also true – light hitting electrons can be absorbed and cause them to be excited.

As anyone who has looked at a rainbow will tell you, not all light is the same – it is composed of lots of different colours.

Some, such as red, have long wavelengths. Others, such as violet, have short wavelengths.

The same is true of the light emitted or absorbed by electrons. Each element has a unique set of wavelengths.

When astronomers study light coming from a distant star, they use instruments to split the light into its spectrum and display it as a series of lines – a bit like a barcode. From this they can work out what the star is made of.

SPECTRUM OF LIGHT

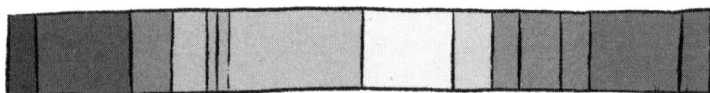

Helium in Sun's atmosphere absorbs light at only set frequencies – leaving lines in the spectrum. (A bit hard to see in grayscale!)

When Janssen looked at the atmosphere of the Sun, there was something wrong with the spectral lines. Some of them were in places they shouldn't be – in places that did not correspond to a known element.

There were, he said, "Two spectra, composed of five or six very bright lines, red, yellow, green, blue and violet."

Janssen made the only deduction he considered reasonable. There was an unknown element.

That element was called helium, after "helios", which is Greek for sun.

How did the world receive his discovery? It laughed!

How could there be an element that existed in that quantity, that we did not know about? Whenever scientists made some new concoction they would joke to each other, "that's helium".

Janssen continued his career, disbelieved – but also gloriously undeterred.

He went to Japan to watch Venus travelling in front of the Sun, he climbed Mont Blanc to see the stars through a thinner atmosphere.

During the Franco-Prussian War, when Paris was besieged, he fled the city in a balloon in order to see another eclipse. On that occasion, the clouds did not break and, despite his derring-do, he missed it.

Still though, no further evidence came for his helium.

The reason why would only become clear almost 30 years later. No one had noticed it because helium is so light.

Whenever it is made on Earth it just drifts off, escaping into the upper atmosphere and space.

Which, Janssen would have been pleased to know, makes it excellent for ballooning.

HUBBLE

You have to be careful with spectroscopy. Edwin Hubble, the astronomer, was very excited one night to spot a galaxy that seemed to be rich in potassium.

After much puzzling, he realized his equipment had picked up the potassium in the match he used to light his pipe.

Almost forty years after his death, a piece of equipment was created that would make no such errors. Hubble had a telescope named after him, and it was sent into space.

On board was a "spectrograph". It was able to analyze the chemical composition of distant galaxies and near planets, becoming the first device to spot that Jupiter's moon Europa was emitting plumes of water.

So precise and powerful was it that, if it had been turned around and pointed at the Earth, it could have well spotted Edwin Hubble lighting a match.

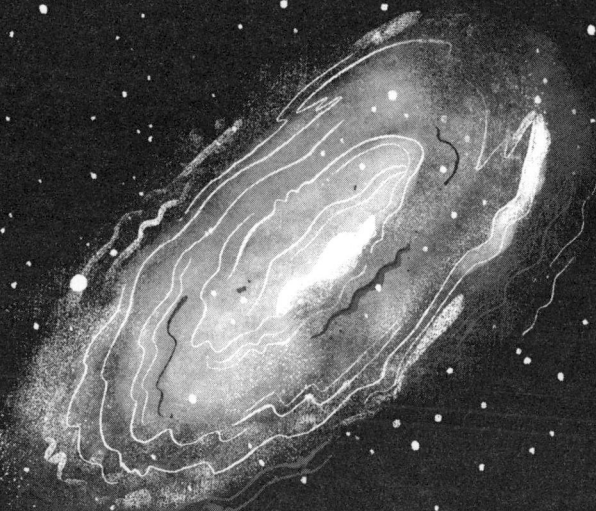

IN SHORT: As Sherlock Holmes said, in a rule that relates as well to detecting metallic compounds as malevolent murderers, "We balance probabilities and choose the most likely. It is the scientific use of the imagination."

WHAT YOU NEED TO KNOW

- Chemists have devised many ways of working out which chemicals are in unknown substances.
- Chromatography involves dissolving a substance in water, dipping paper in, and watching how the different components separate as they rise up the paper.
- Flame tests work because when different metal compounds burn, they make different colours.
- Spectroscopy takes advantage of the fact that a vaporized element emits light at specific wavelengths – which show up as characteristic lines in the light spectrum.

TIME-TRAVELLING CHEMISTRY, PART 8: REFRIGERATION

Clare's water is clean. She has a cup to drink it out of. She doesn't smell. And, looking out across the prehistoric sunset, she thinks with satisfaction that she and the Stone Agers are now in charge of all they survey.

And yet, something still niggles. Wouldn't it be nice, she muses, if the water was chilled?

Yes, indeed it would. But how would that be possible without electricity?

The answer is, the same way it was possible for the ancient Egyptians.

Ancient scrolls show Egyptian slaves fanning pottery jars. Some scientists think they know why: they had pot-in-pot refrigerators.

Pot-in-pot refrigerators cool things for the same reason sweat cools things – they use evaporation.

When water evaporates, changing from liquid to vapour, it takes heat energy out of the surface it is on. So when you sweat, the liquid evaporates and cools your skin.

The reason you feel even colder if it is windy is that the wind helps to blow away newly-vaporised air molecules, allowing others to evaporate and take their place.

The pot-in-pot refrigerator is a way of making a pot of water sweat.

What it requires is a big pot which isn't glazed – which means water will seep through it – and a smaller pot, which is glazed.

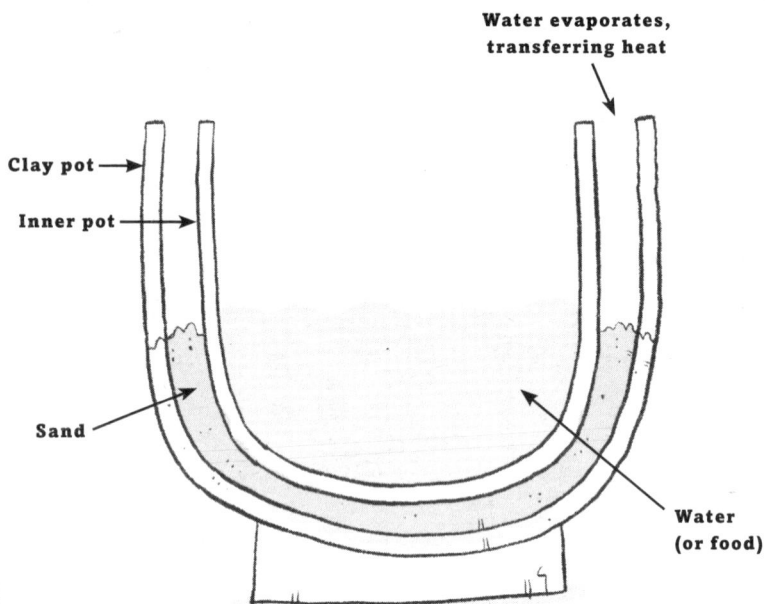

Water evaporates, transferring heat

Clay pot

Inner pot

Sand

Water (or food)

Sipping, at last, a cool glass of water, Clare wonders, is this finally it? Is it time to rest?

No, she thinks. There is one last great chemical advance to gift the Stone Agers, to ensure that her name and deeds echo in eternity...

CHAPTER 9

THE ATMOSPHERE AND THE ENVIRONMENT

INTRODUCTION
THE ATMOSPHERE AND THE ENVIRONMENT

IN THIS CHAPTER YOU WILL LEARN ABOUT:

- The composition of the atmosphere
- The greenhouse effect
- The Haber process

BEFORE YOU READ THIS CHAPTER:

We don't think about air much.

We think about water every day – especially when the weather's hot. We think about food even more: we buy books about it, talk about it, and watch daytime television shows about it.

There are no daytime television shows, though, about air. This is despite the fact that you can survive days without water and weeks without food, but just minutes without air.

The atmosphere is not just there, like a mountain. It is an ever-changing, ever-recycling balance of gases – that can sustain or destroy life. Several times in the deep past, the balance has gone wrong, and mass extinction has been the result.

This chapter is about three of the gases currently rushing in and out of your lungs; the three gases that, directly and indirectly, keep you alive.

One is oxygen, taken from the lungs and transported by blood cells around your body to keep it running.

The other is carbon dioxide, which, in barely-perceptible quantities, keeps the world warm enough that that your blood does not freeze.

The third is nitrogen, without which, plants could never provide the energy that we need to survive – energy which the oxygen in your blood helps unlock.

The tale of these gases is not simple, and their continued existence in the precise proportions we have today is not guaranteed.

So maybe we should stop ignoring them.

EVOLUTION OF THE ATMOSPHERE: THE RISE OF OXYGEN

Oxygen, for us, is the stuff of life. For most of the history of the Earth, though, it was either not present at all – or deadly. The story of the rise of humans is also the story of the rise of oxygen.

TIMELINE:*

4.5 billion years ago: The Earth is formed, and it's not a place you'd want to live on. It is impossible to know for certain what gases were in the atmosphere – but we do know there was none of the oxygen we need to breathe.

4.3 bya: Continual volcanic eruptions release large quantities of carbon dioxide and water vapour.

4 bya: The Earth cools, allowing water vapour to condense and form oceans, which absorb some of the carbon dioxide to make carbonate compounds – which eventually formed rocks.

3.4 bya: Plants learn to convert sunlight and CO_2 into energy (a process called photosynthesis) – but produce sulphur as a by-product.

2.7 bya: A new kind of photosynthesis develops, that instead makes oxygen – which grows to become a quarter of the atmosphere.

2.3 bya: This new toxic gas, oxygen, increases in concentration and begins to kill off bacteria.

2–1.5 bya: Other life evolves which, instead of being killed by oxygen, can use it to breathe.

0.6 bya: Organisms take advantage of the efficiency of breathing using oxygen to grow bigger and faster – they are called animals.

Percentages of carbon dioxide and oxygen in the Earth's atmosphere over time

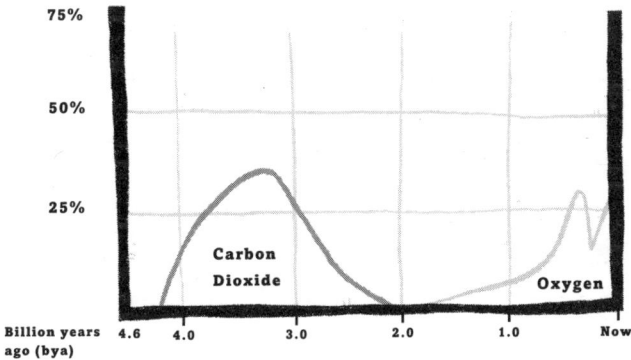

75%
50%
25%

Carbon Dioxide

Oxygen

Billion years ago (bya)   4.6   4.0   3.0   2.0   1.0   Now

* There were no people around for most of this time – and there were even fewer atmospheric chemists. So, much of this is an educated guess!

THE CARBON CYCLE AND CLIMATE CHANGE

One of the largest extinctions ever began with a burp.

About 55 million years ago, 10 million years after the dinosaurs disappeared, something strange happened to the Earth's atmosphere. Its carbon dioxide levels suddenly shot up.

Why this, an event referred to by scientists as "The Big Burp", occurred remains open to debate.

One of the more plausible theories is that undersea volcanic activity led to a warming of the oceans, which itself led to the release of lots of methane – which then reacted to become CO_2.

But if the cause is unknown, the effect is not. In a time period that, from a geological point of view, is essentially instantaneous, the temperature soared by 5 degrees Celsius – and stayed that way for 100,000 years.

Carbon dioxide is a greenhouse gas. Greenhouse gases – which also include water vapour and methane – are a good thing. They are the reason the Earth is a place humans can live in, rather than a place they freeze to death in. They work by reflecting the Sun's heat back onto the Earth. When the energy from the Sun travels through space, it does so as something called **short-wave radiation**.

This travels easily through the atmosphere, and

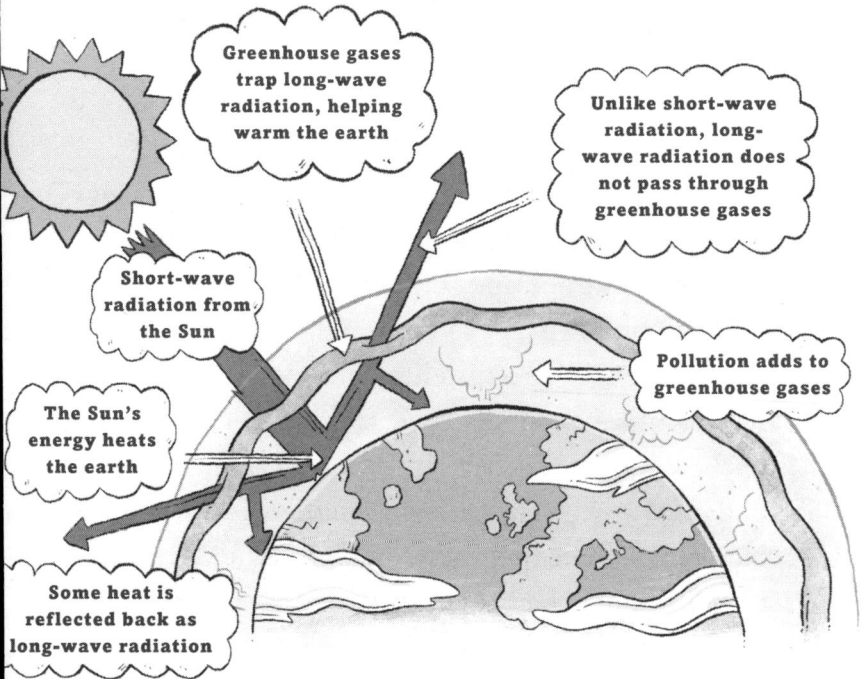

Greenhouse gases trap long-wave radiation, helping warm the earth

Unlike short-wave radiation, long-wave radiation does not pass through greenhouse gases

Short-wave radiation from the Sun

Pollution adds to greenhouse gases

The Sun's energy heats the earth

Some heat is reflected back as long-wave radiation

when it reaches the Earth, it warms it up. Some of this heat from the Earth is itself radiated into space, and it does so as a different kind of radiation – not shortwave, like that from the Sun, but **longwave**. This kind of radiation is a bit different: it does not travel at all easily through the atmosphere. Instead, it gets stopped by greenhouse gases.

Greenhouse gases have a cunning trick. They are transparent to short-wave radiation, but not longwave radiation. When the short-wave kind hits the Earth and bounces back as the long-wave kind, suddenly it is trapped – and reflected back down from the atmosphere again.

In this way, the Earth remains permanently above the temperature it should be, if it didn't have greenhouse gases. Without the greenhouse effect, we would average an exceedingly chilly –18 degrees Celsius, rather than +15 degrees Celsius.

This was what happened 55 million years ago. Suddenly, billions of tonnes of CO_2 found its way into the atmosphere, began reflecting back the short-wave radiation – and cooked the planet.

In the Arctic, which warmed the most, sea temperatures reached 23 degrees Celsius – enough for tropical snorkelling.

For the creatures living there, who definitely had not adapted to tropical snorkelling, this wasn't good.

Among those animals living on the seafloor, this temperature rise was worse than the asteroid that killed the dinosaurs – as many as half went extinct.

The good news is, events like as the Big Burp are rare.

The bad news is, we are busily creating one.

According to recent estimates, during the height of the burp, the world emitted 500 million tonnes of CO_2 a year.

Human industry is currently emitting 20 times that, and despite efforts to reduce that, in much of the world CO_2 output is still increasing.

Less a burp – more an almighty belch.

THE HABER PROCESS

In 1934, when the German chemist Fritz Haber died, where did he go?

As he stood at the pearly gates, awaiting judgement, which way did the scales fall – heaven or hell?

If you are known as the "Father of chemical warfare", if you led Germany's poison gas programme and enthusiastically recruited fellow scientists to join you in the First World War's greatest atrocities, then it should seem pretty clear where you are going to spend eternity.

And Haber would not have needed a jumper when he got there.

Yet, arguably, Haber was also responsible for the existence of most of the world's population – thanks to the chemical technique that now bears his name.

There is a good case to be made that the Haber process is the most significant invention of the twentieth century ... and also the least appreciated.

Unlike computers or space rockets or aeroplanes, it barely

impacts on most people's conscious lives, but half of the nitrogen in you is there as a result of it.

The Haber process is a way of making **ammonia**, which is used in plant fertilizer. Without this, and the huge-scale production of food which it makes possible, the world would simply be unable to sustain the population it currently has.

Haber's insight was to find a way to react nitrogen and hydrogen to make NH_3 – ammonia – in industrial quantities.

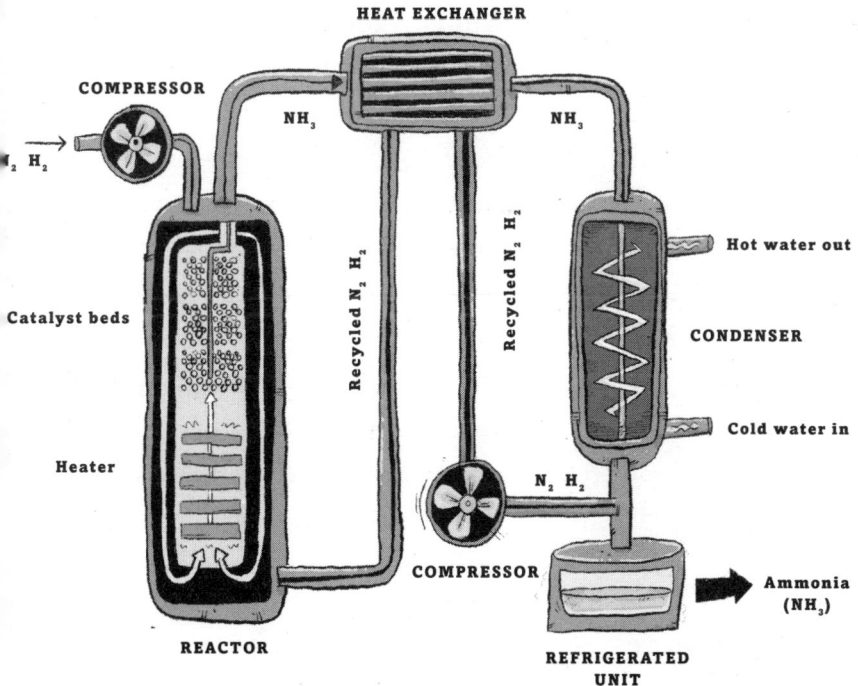

Ammonia is important, because plants can use it to get nitrogen. And they need nitrogen, because, without it, they can't make the cells that convert sunlight into energy.

Before Haber, the most plentiful source of nitrogen fertilizers was bird poo (as our Stone Age chemist used to her advantage in Chapter Five).

Whole economies in South America were built on mining centuries of accumulated bird poo from islands in the Pacific.

The problem was, the birds weren't pooing fast enough. Based on the quantities available, Victorians believed that the world's population was doomed to collapse.

Once bird poo went, they thought, crops would die – and so would we.

But the Haber process makes a lot more ammonia than birds. Today, factories manufacture more than 150 million tonnes every year, using the Haber process.

The process is the reason that the world can support a population many billions higher than the level that Victorians had thought possible.

So, without the Haber process, half of us would die.

(Take that, Saint Peter.)

THOMAS MIDGLEY

Thomas Midgley was both a very good and very bad inventor.

He was good, because he came up with innovations that changed the lives of every person on the planet.

He was bad, because they tended to do so by making those lives a lot worse.

In October 1924, Midgley held a press conference. Some reporters were already asking if his latest invention – an extra chemical ingredient to make petrol engines run more smoothly – might also have some rather unpleasant side effects.

In a dramatic flourish, Midgley proved them wrong. He took a jar of tetraethyl lead, the chemical in question, and poured it over his hands. Then he sniffed it.

See, he said – completely safe.

It is difficult to believe he did not, even then, know the truth. In the factories that made his chemical people were dying, hallucinating and going mad.

But over the next 70 years, his additive became one of the most important in Chemistry: the world's cars ran on "leaded petrol".

The result, scientists now know, is that everyone alive then was slightly poisoned.

Many believe it caused mild brain damage, lowering the world's IQ and even changing behaviours. Only by the 1990s was it phased out.

That would have been enough for most lifetimes, but Midgley's second greatest invention managed to ruin the planet in a completely different way.

This time, at least, he cannot be blamed.

No one could have predicted that **chlorofluorocarbons**, which he developed to make refrigerators more effective, would also do something rather more dramatic.

They would deplete the Earth's ozone layer – the protective shield of ozone gas that deflects dangerous rays from the sun. CFCs, too, were phased out by the end of the century.

Midgley never lived to see the end of either though. He developed polio in the 1940s and, weakened by the illness, came up with his third invention – an intricate system of pulleys to get him out of bed.

Like the inventions that went before, this one had a serious flaw.

Unlike the inventions that came before, only he was the victim: it tangled around his neck and strangled him.

IN SHORT: Don't mess with the atmosphere.

WHAT YOU NEED TO KNOW:

- The Haber process uses heat, pressure and a catalyst to convert nitrogen and hydrogen into ammonia, which plants can use as fertilizer.
- Greenhouse gases, such as carbon dioxide and methane, trap heat by reflecting short-wave radiation. They keep the Earth warm enough for life, but too much greenhouse gas causes climate change.
- The atmosphere today is 78 per cent nitrogen, 21 per cent oxygen, with trace amounts of other gases including carbon dioxide.
- In the early atmosphere, there was a lot more carbon dioxide. This was absorbed into the oceans or into plants using photosynthesis.
- The oxygen level increased, due to expiration by plants.

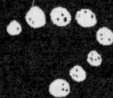

TIME-TRAVELLING CHEMISTRY, PART 9: GUNPOWDER

Was Alexander the Great ever forced to wee on a dung heap, Clare wonders to herself? Did Caesar ever suffer the indignity of spending months adding fresh wee to stale wee, then raking over rotten animal poo?

No, probably not. But, she reminds herself, Caesar got stabbed.

Somewhere along the way, Clare's ambitions have changed.

Being an early farmer was fun. It had its moments. But after the first crop and then the second, she found herself experiencing a certain itchiness. An ambition.

The same ambition that, in a different life, had propelled her to revise so hard for her Chemistry exams.

She finds she wants more for the Stone Agers; a more glorious, noble future.

A future that might just involve the teensiest, weensiest element of… How would she put it?

Ah yes: global conquest.

First, she just has to get the weeing formula right. Because weeing, you see, is not just good for watering the plants; it is also the first step towards something rather more mighty than a flint axe.

So, with renewed vigour and purpose, Clare sends another jet splattering into the dung heap – which has been mixed with straw and ash.

This project, the ultimate project, has been going on for almost a year now. To make her plan work she needed charcoal ... but that's not a problem.

She also needed sulphur ... but this, the cradle of humanity, is a volcanic region. Sulphur is plentiful.

The third ingredient though is something far more elusive: saltpetre.

Saltpetre, also known as potassium nitrate (KNO_3), is an oxidizer. When it gets hot, it does not use up oxygen – it makes it. It decomposes and releases this gas.

$$2KNO_3 \gg 2KNO_2 + O_2$$

And saltpetre is exactly what Clare needs – so she gets weeing.

After a few months of weeing and raking, weeing and raking, something magical happens. From her urine-soaked dung heap comes a layer of white crystals.

This, Clare's dung heap harvest, is what she was waiting for.

She is not quite done though. These crystals have a lot of saltpetre in, but not enough.

Dissolve them in water, filter the whole solution through more wood ash, leave it to dry in the sun and the concentration is, probably, just about high enough.

Excited, Clare crushes up the white crystals. Carefully, she mixes them with finely-ground charcoal and sulphur – roughly 10 per cent sulphur, 15 per cent charcoal and 75 per cent saltpetre.

Then she stands back and, with a very long splint, sets fire to it.

What happens next, happens fast. The charcoal and sulphur, as she would expect, set on fire – they oxidize.

But when they do, they heat up the saltpetre, which releases oxygen. Rather than being limited by how much oxygen it can recruit from the air, the mixture now makes its own oxygen.

It burns faster and faster.

Or, in other words, it explodes.

Temporarily dazzled, Clare's eyes slowly readjust.

Smiling, she looks across the landscape of a different world – a world she controls, a world that will shudder before her might and majesty.

She has made gunpowder.

THE
SCIENCE NEWS

ARCHAEOLOGISTS FIND 250,000 YEAR-OLD CIVILIZATION

Archaeologists yesterday announced they had excavated a human civilization predating our own by at least 260,000 years.

Describing the find as "spectacular, and spectacularly baffling," they said that they had uncovered pottery shards and signs of agriculture from a time hundreds of thousands of years before humans were meant to have developed either technology.

Professor Joanna Boffin said that the find could rewrite our understanding of human evolution.

"There are simply not meant to be these technologies at this time," she said. "This goes against everything that we know about the course of our development.

"Here we have sophisticated Chemistry and Engineering in one isolated spot in Africa. But at the time, we had barely come into existence as a species.

"This is like finding an iPhone in Ancient Greece.

"One of the strangest finds was a nested series of pots. A colleague insisted it would have worked like a primitive fridge but that seemed too fantastical – who would bother chilling water at a time when the species was battling just to survive?"

Scientists said the two biggest questions yet to be answered are, firstly: How did this isolated group of humans develop technology so early? And, secondly: what happened to them?

"The only clue to their fate is in the last layer of sediment," said Professor Boffin. "It seems to be heavily scorched and rich in potassium compounds, as if there was a large fire or even – and this is utterly ridiculous – an explosion."

According to the professor, we may never know the real answer.

WHY CHEMISTRY MATTERS

WHY CHEMISTRY MATTERS

If you've read this book from end to end, you've now covered most of the essentials for your Chemistry exam – but you've also glimpsed the science that falls outside of your school syllabus.

And at the end of all of that, you might just think… So what? What does it matter?

Chemistry is about atoms, and atoms are very small. So much smaller than you can see; so much smaller than you can ever imagine. Why do you need to know this?

The answer – or at least *an* answer – might just come in the room that John Goodenough surveyed, when he came to visit Britain in the autumn of 2019. Professor Goodenough was there to receive a prize known as the Copley Medal, awarded for his work in lithium Chemistry.

The Copley Medal is the oldest scientific award in the world. It has been given by the Royal Society, the world's oldest scientific academy, since the 1700s. Past recipients include Charles Darwin and Robert Bunsen (yes, of burner fame). It is not, in other words, a prize that is easily upstaged.

But on that morning, as the 98 year-old chemist looked out over the Royal Society's library, upstaged it was. Just as he was poised to pick up the Copley, Professor Goodenough received a call from Sweden, telling him he had won the Nobel Prize too.

It seemed like, suddenly, everyone was extremely interested in the Chemistry of lithium ions. "What is so special about lithium?" asked the journalists who assembled for the event – each holding up voice recorders whose power source relied on lithium.

"Why," repeated the TV crews, "should we care about this element?" Awaiting his answer, they pointed cameras that were, even then, working by moving lithium ions from one electrode to another.

Over 30 years earlier, Professor Goodenough had, through Chemistry, helped create one of the most revolutionary inventions in the history of the world: the lithium ion battery. Without it, there would be no mobile phones, laptops or tablets.

Every day, all over the world, trillions upon trillions of lithium ions, in millions upon millions of devices, move slowly from one side of a battery to another.

Then, once they have all gone one way, they are plugged in – and transfer in the other direction, ready to be used again. They allow us to take electricity on the move, with an efficiency never before possible.

And although John Goodenough received the prize, many women and men were responsible.

There were the scientists who first categorised the elements, and those who began to understand what ions were. There were the Victorians who developed electrochemistry, and those who discovered how to harness it. Together, they created a revolution.

They were also people, like you. So, while you cram for your exams, keep in mind that Chemistry isn't just a subject of dry equations. It's a subject created by people who wanted to understand not just how the world works, but also why.

But that morning, that was not the answer that Professor Goodenough gave, when asked about the impact of his work. Instead, he took his hand and tapped gently on the left side of his chest.

Inside, there was a pacemaker. Some years earlier he had had heart problems, that nearly killed him. He was alive because dozens of times a minute this pacemaker provided a little pulse of electricity that kept his heart in time.

And, he explained that morning, it was powered by lithium. His Chemistry had brought him fame; it had also saved his life.

APPENDIX:
THE
PERIODIC
TABLE

PERIODIC TABLE OF ELEMENTS

1 **2**

Atomic number → | 1 **H** Hydrogen 1 | ← Element symbol
← Element name

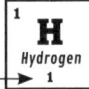

Relative atomic mass →

1 **H** Hydrogen 1								
3 **Li** Lithium 6.9	4 **Be** Beryllium 9.0							
11 **Na** Sodium 23.0	12 **Mg** Magnesium 24.3							
19 **K** Potassium 39.1	20 **Ca** Calcium 40.1	21 **Sc** Scandium 45.0	22 **Ti** Titanium 47.9	23 **V** Vanadium 50.9	24 **Cr** Chromium 52.0	25 **Mn** Manganese 54.9	26 **Fe** Iron 55.8	27 **C** Cob 58
37 **Rb** Rubidium 85.5	38 **Sr** Strontium 87.6	39 **Y** Yttrium 88.9	40 **Zr** Zirconium 91.2	41 **Nb** Niobium 92.9	42 **Mo** Molybdenum 96.0	43 **Tc** Technetium [97]	44 **Ru** Ruthenium 101.1	45 **R** Rho 10
55 **Cs** Caesium 132.9	56 **Ba** Barium 137.3	57-71 **La** Lanthanides	72 **Hf** Hafnium 178.5	73 **Ta** Tantalum 180.9	74 **W** Tungsten 183.8	75 **Re** Rhenium 186.2	76 **Os** Osmium 190.2	77 **I** Iric 192
87 **Fr** Francium [223]	88 **Ra** Radium [226]	89-103 **Ac** Actinides	104 **Rf** Rutherfordium [267]	105 **Db** Dubnium [270]	106 **Sg** Seaborgium [269]	107 **Bh** Bohrium [270]	108 **Hs** Hassium [270]	109 **M** Meitr [2

57 **La** Lanthanum [138.9]	58 **Ce** Cerium 140.1	59 **Pr** Praseodymium 140.9	60 **Nd** Neodymium 144.2	61 **Pm** Promethium [145]	62 **Sm** Samarium 150.4	63 **E** Eur 15
89 **Ac** Actinium [227]	90 **Th** Thorium 232.0	91 **Pa** Protactinium 231.0	92 **U** Uranium 238.0	93 **Np** Neptunium [237]	94 **Pu** Plutonium [244]	95 **A** Ame [2

| 3 | 4 | 5 | 6 | 7 | 0 |

| | | | | | 2 **He** Helium 2 |

1

| 5 **B** Boron 10.8 | 6 **C** Carbon 12.0 | 7 **N** Nitrogen 14.0 | 8 **O** Oxygen 16.0 | 9 **F** Fluorine 19.0 | 10 **Ne** Neon 20.2 |

| 13 **Al** Aluminium 27.0 | 14 **Ca** Silicon 28.1 | 15 **P** Phosphorus 31.0 | 16 **S** Sulphur 32.1 | 17 **Cl** Chlorine 35.5 | 18 **Ar** Argon 39.9 |

| 29 **Cu** Copper 63.5 | 30 **Zn** Zinc 65.4 | 31 **Ga** Gallium 69.7 | 32 **Ge** Germanium 72.6 | 33 **As** Arsenic 74.9 | 34 **Se** Selenium 79.0 | 35 **Br** Bromine 79.9 | 36 **Kr** Krypton 83.8 |

Ni Nickel 58.7

| 47 **Ag** Silver 107.9 | 48 **Cd** Cadmium 112.4 | 49 **In** Indium 114.8 | 50 **Sn** Tin 118.7 | 51 **Sb** Antimony 121.8 | 52 **Te** Tellurium 127.6 | 53 **I** Iodine 126.9 | 54 **Xe** Xenon 131.3 |

Pd Palladium 106.4

| 79 **Au** Gold 197.0 | 80 **Mg** Mercury 200.6 | 81 **Tl** Thallium 204.4 | 82 **Pb** Lead 207.2 | 83 **Bi** Bismuth 209.0 | 84 **Po** Polonium [209] | 85 **At** Astatine [210] | 86 **Rn** Radon [222] |

Pt Platinum 195.1

| 111 **Rg** Roentgenium [281] | 112 **Cn** Copernicium [285] | 113 **Nh** Nihonium [286] | 114 **Fl** Flerovium [289] | 115 **Mc** Moscovium [289] | 116 **Lv** Livermorium [293] | 117 **Ts** Tennessine [294] | 118 **Og** Oganesson [294] |

Ds Darmstadtium [281]

| 65 **Tb** Terbium 158.9 | 66 **Dy** Dysprosium 162.5 | 67 **Ho** Holmium 164.9 | 68 **Er** Erbium 167.3 | 69 **Tm** Thulium 168.9 | 70 **Yb** Ytterbium 173.0 | 71 **Lu** Lutetium Protactinium 175.0 |

d nium 7.3

| 97 **Bk** Berkelium [247] | 98 **Cf** Californium [251] | 99 **Es** Einsteinium [252] | 100 **Fm** Fermium [257] | 101 **Md** Mendelevium [258] | 102 **No** Nobelium [259] | 103 **Lr** Lawrencium [262] |

m um 7]

PERIODIC TABLE GROUPS

METALS

Most elements are metals. Metals are generally strong, conduct heat and electricity and have high melting points – meaning they are solid at room temperature. They lose their outer electrons easily when they react (see Chapter Two for more).

H																	He
Li	Be											B	C	N	O	F	Ne
Na	Mg											Al	Si	P	S	Cl	Ar
K	Ca	Sc	Ti	V	Cr	Mn	Fe	Co	Ni	Cu	Zn	Ga	Ge	As	Se	Br	Kr
Rb	Sr	Y	Zr	Nb	Mo	Tc	Ru	Rh	Pd	Ag	Cd	In	Sn	Sb	Te	I	Xe
Cs	Ba	La	Hr	Ta	W	Re	Os	Ir	Pt	Au	Hg	Tl	Pb	Bi	Po	At	Rn
Fr	Ra	Ac	Rf	Db	Sg	Bh	Hs	Mt	Ds	Rg	Cn	Nh	Fl	Mc	Lv	Ts	Og

■ METALS   NON-METALS

GROUP 0 (THE NOBLE GASES)

With 8 electrons in a full outer shell (or two in the case of helium), these elements have no wish to pick up or lose other electrons, so rarely react. The further down group 0 you go, the higher the boiling point – but they all still have very low boiling points.

																	H																	He
Li	Be											B	C	N	Ó	F	Ne
Na	Mg											Al	Si	P	S	Cl	Ar
K	Ca	Sc	Ti	V	Cr	Mn	Fe	Co	Ni	Cu	Zn	Ga	Ge	As	Se	Br	Kr
Rb	Sr	Y	Zr	Nb	Mo	Tc	Ru	Rh	Pd	Ag	Cd	In	Sn	Sb	Te	I	Xe
Cs	Ba	La	Hr	Ta	W	Re	Os	Ir	Pt	Au	Hg	Tl	Pb	Bi	Po	At	Rn
Fr	Ra	Ac	Rf	Db	Sg	Bh	Hs	Mt	Ds	Rg	Cn	Nh	Fl	Mc	Lv	Ts	Og

■ GROUP 0 (THE NOBLE GASES)

GROUP 1 (THE ALKALI METALS)

These metals all have 1 electron in their outer shell. It's very easy for them to lose 1 electron, which means they react easily – as anyone who has thrown potassium in a sink will know (don't throw potassium in a sink!).

When that potassium (or any of these metals) reacts with water, it makes a hydroxide (e.g. potassium hydroxide, KOH) and hydrogen. They also react easily with oxygen to make metal oxides.

The further down the group you go, the more reactive they get – because the outermost electron is further from the nucleus, so it is easier for it to escape.

GROUP 1 (THE ALKALI METALS)

GROUP 7 (THE HALOGENS)

These elements are all one electron short of a full outer shell – meaning they like to gain an electron, to make a full shell and bond with metals. For instance sodium and chlorine come together to make sodium chloride, or salt.

As you go down, and there are more shells of electrons, the halogens become less reactive, and have higher melting and boiling points.

Sometimes, in chemical reactions, a more reactive halogen will displace a less reactive one. For instance: **chlorine + potassium iodide » potassium chloride + iodine.** (The halogens have just swapped places.)

GROUP 7 (THE HALOGENS)

TRANSITION METALS

Unlike the metals in group 1, these have very high melting points, and are typically very strong, dense and hard. They are also less reactive.

TRANSITION METALS

**** BEFORE YOU SEND US LETTERS ****

Here are a small number of reasons why all that was wrong:

[*1] Alright, not hydrogen – which has no neutrons.

[*2] This is, by the by, equivalent to assuming (for the purposes of simplicity) that Hitler can be understood as a man who got a bit cross at the world because it didn't like his paintings. It might contain an element of truth, but it wouldn't exactly get you far in GCSE History.

In reality, this familiar description of an atom does not begin to touch on its weirdness. While most diagrams of atoms show the electron buzzing around its nucleus, if drawn to scale, in order to have both the electron and nucleus on the same piece of A4 they would both be so small they'd be invisible.

If the nucleus was instead the size of a basketball, the first electron would be almost 13,000 km away – that's the distance across the Earth.

So, the atom is almost entirely empty space. Except … it's not at all because the electrons are not fixed points, they are "fuzzy" waves spread diffusely along their orbit.

Oh, and some of the orbits don't orbit the nucleus at all.

[*3] Actually, the third shell accepts up to 18, but ten are hidden away. They come into play in the sixth pedant point.

[*4] With the exception of the platypus and echidna which are mammals that lay eggs.

[*5] You might have guessed by now, but they're not quite that simple. In fact, the atomic masses given in the Periodic Table are ever so slightly different from these numbers.

[*6] You will notice that the groups are labelled 0 to 7, but after three rows a rather large, unlabelled, group inserts itself in the way. These are the transition metals, and they exist because of those annoying hidden ten electron spaces. In these metals, these extra spaces are filled up – and everything gets a lot less neat.

One reason is neutrons and protons don't weigh exactly the same. The other reason is a little bit of mass is held in the energy that binds them together – calculated using Einstein's formula $E = mc^2$.

The final reason why (which doesn't require understanding complex theoretical Physics and Einstein's mass-energy equivalence) is explained in the isotopes section in Chapter One.

INDEX

INDEX

TOM WHIPPLE is the science editor at *The Times*. His career has taken him to the top of Mont Blanc and to the tunnels beneath CERN. He has investigated the effects of radiation in the forests around Chernobyl, and the effects of heat in the world's hottest sauna in Finland. He didn't stay in very long. He has reported on three climate change conferences, and only been arrested at one of them. He has a mathematics degree.

JAMES DAVIES is an illustrator and author from deepest darkest Wales, but he now lives in Bristol. He works on all kinds of fun projects and spends all his time drawing explosions, goblins and farting cows. It's his absolute dream. When he's not working, he can be found eating cheese and getting attacked by his cat.

ACKNOWLEDGMENTS

So many times in writing this book, I have mentally travelled back to my own school days, to the men and women who first tried to explain these concepts to me.

The memory of teachers inevitably stays longer, and sharper, in a child's mind than the child does in the teacher's. Most, probably, will have long forgotten me – but I have not forgotten them, or (some of) the things they taught me.

In making the shift in this book from pupil to teacher, I realized how hard their job is – and how well so many of them did it. So I would like to thank them all, in particular Mr Sharma, Mr Cousins, Mr Perkins and Mr Oakes (teachers, even 25 years on, should not have first names), who guided me through GCSE science, mathematics and beyond. Shane Henry, a good friend who became a good chemistry teacher, kindly proofread the book. So too did Mary Kerr – Chemistry examiner, Chemistry teacher with a minor crush on Dmitri Mendeleev and, last but not least, aunt. What they missed was picked up by the diligent eye of Helen Mortimer. Any mistakes, naturally, are my own.

I would also like to thank Denise Johnstone-Burt and Jane Winterbotham at Walker Books, who came up with the idea, and Jamie Hammond, who was able to make it beautiful in a way that would have entirely eluded me. Talking of beauty, the wonderful illustrations come from James Davies.

The measure of a good editor is that, when you receive their notes and corrections, you should first believe them to be stupid, then actively malevolent then finally – a few hours later – accept that they were right all along. Becky Watson is a very good editor, and I thank her for her persistence, diligence and unwillingness to let a confusing sentence pass.

Sarah Williams, my agent, continues to corral some fairly eclectic ideas into a form that people might actually want to buy. Her support and advice has been invaluable.

The Times allows me the ridiculous privilege of employing me to chat each day to scientists about their work.

Finally, I would like to thank Catherine. A two-author household that has in the past six years produced twice as many books as children (and hasn't stinted on the children) is not without its stresses. Because of Catherine it has been a collaborative adventure that we have enjoyed together.

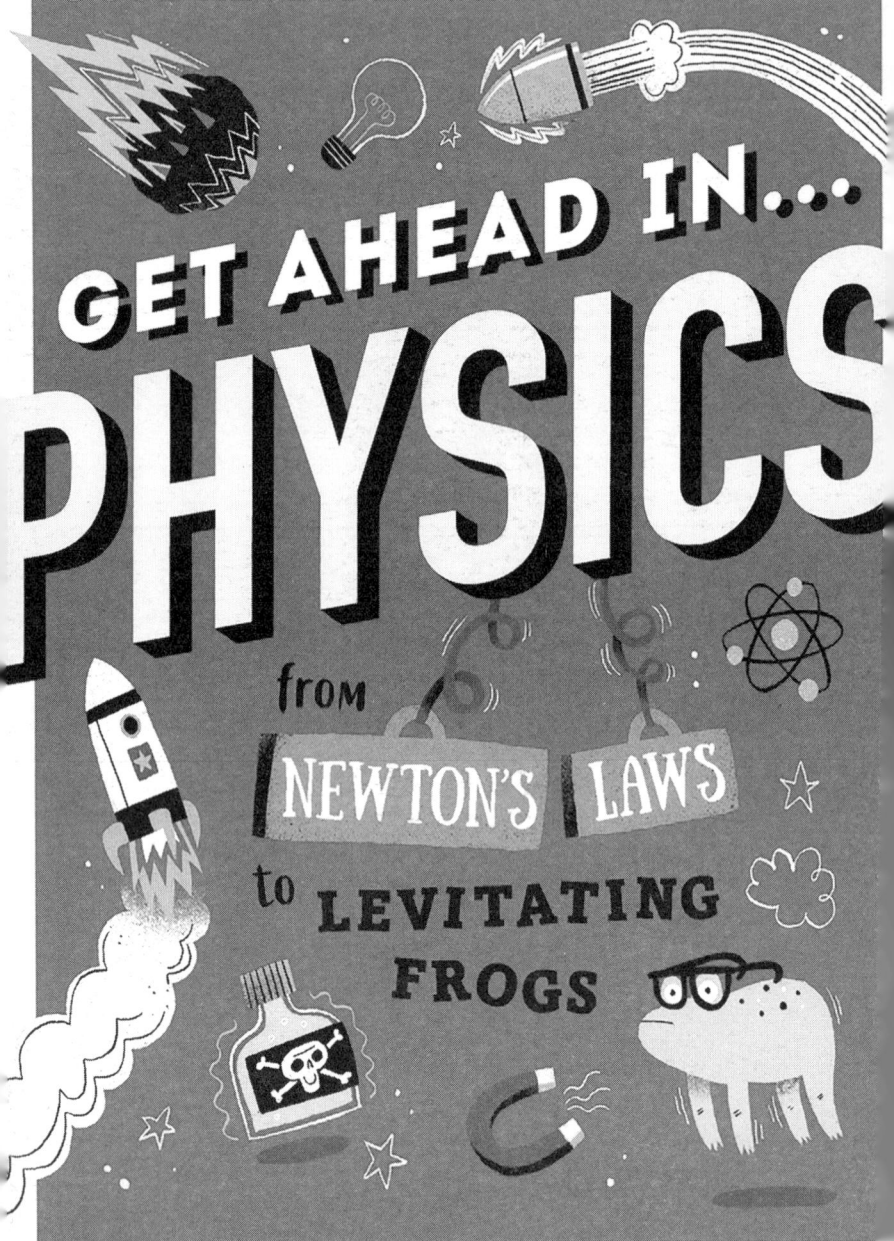